Dying Twice

Dying Twice

A Sister's Tale

EMMA DALLY

LITTLE, BROWN AND COMPANY

A *Little, Brown* Book

First published in Great Britain in 2000
by Little, Brown and Company

Copyright © Emma Dally, 2000

The moral right of the author has been asserted.

A CIP catalogue record for this book
is available from the British Library.

ISBN 0 316 85322 4

Typeset in Janson by M Rules
Printed and bound in Great Britain by
Clays Ltd, St Ives plc

Little, Brown and Company (UK)
Brettenham House
Lancaster Place
London WC2E 7EN

For R.M.E.

Acknowledgements

I am grateful to many people for giving me stories about John to include in this account. All the members of my family have been helpful. My mother, always a good storyteller, came up with some vivid vignettes of John's childhood. My brother Adam provided valuable details about his and John's young adult lives as well as the last weeks. My sister Jane, brother Mark and sister-in-law Clare, all contributed some good stories over which we still chuckle. Paul Chauveau produced priceless accounts of life at St Christopher's, and Imogen Bloor was immeasurably helpful with her perceptive observations of John as both her friend and patient.

Jacques is a central character in this drama and I was keen to talk to him about the events of 1994. I put out feelers in the hope of getting a contribution but sadly the response was unequivocally negative. This is a shame but I bear Jacques no ill will.

Thanks, too, to Alan Samson, my editor at Little, Brown, for his sensitive suggestions and editing.

Most of all I should like to thank my husband, Richard Ehrlich, who contributed memories and analysis as well as the usual support and firm editorial advice.

PART ONE

Waiting to Die

Chapter One

December 1993

As the year 1993 was drawing to an end, I was on a high. I had just about recovered from the birth of our third child and was beginning to feel that life was normal again. I enjoyed my job as deputy editor on *She* magazine, where I had been working for three years, and I had recently received an offer from a book publisher for two novels to be written over the next three years. Also I had just won first prize in the charity raffle at the British Society of Magazine Editors' dinner: a two-week holiday for two in south-east Asia which included stays at the Oriental Hotels in Bangkok and Singapore, a luxury cruise around the islands of Thailand and a trip on the Eastern and Oriental Express.

Life seemed great. I had plenty to look forward to in the coming year. The raffle prize was valid for twelve months, so my husband, Dick, and I decided to take off for Thailand the following November, when Ruth would be two and a half.

Our older daughters, Rebecca and Alice, were now 7½ and 6 respectively.

Four days after winning that raffle, however, everything changed. Instead of looking forward to a new and successful year, we were suddenly catapulted towards a nightmare from which there was no escape. As we hurtled into it, there was no way of knowing exactly what lay ahead of us, what horrors we were to witness, or how long it would last.

Worst of all was the knowledge that we would only finally be released from this intolerable situation with another death in the family. Even then it could be only a partial release, as the effects would last for ever.

Early December. I come back to my desk after lunch to find messages that both my father and my youngest brother, Adam, have telephoned. I immediately know that this is about my family as my father hardly ever rings me at home, let alone work, and Adam (who lives in New York) has asked me to return his call urgently. Since my family is large and extended there is always something happening to somebody and I sense that this is something bad.

As I am looking up Adam's business number in New York, he calls again. 'John's in the Middlesex Hospital.' His voice has that transatlantic echo. 'He flew over yesterday and was admitted straight away. He's got PCP, and it's bad, but they think they've caught it in time. He's lucky. It's dangerous to fly with pneumonia because there's a risk of having a collapsed lung from the pressure in the plane. I've called Peter.'

Peter is my father. He chose to be called by that name by his children, not Dad or anything so sentimental. This explains the call from him.

'Where is he? Which ward?'

'Ring Jacques. He and Paul took John in yesterday. It's the HIV-AIDS ward, the Charles Bell.'

Jacques is John's ex-partner; Paul is an old schoolfriend. I have not seen either of them for years.

There is nothing more to say. Adam's voice sounds distant and urgent. It must be fairly early in the morning over there in New York. And cold.

I put down the telephone and spread my hands over my face. I long to hide away somewhere; but if I get up and walk across the office towards the lavatory, I know I shall burst into tears and I don't wish the entire staff of the magazine to see me in such a state.

The ladies' lavatory is the traditional refuge for sobbing female employees of the National Magazine Company – usually people who have been shouted at by their boss. Some years there are more than others, depending on the managerial skills of the editors and publishers. Fortunately, on *She* there are generally few tears. Under Linda Kelsey's editorship, it is a well-managed and happy place.

Linda is a good friend. I have worked with her for seven years now – first on *Cosmopolitan* where she was editor, and I was both literary and assistant editor, and since 1990 on *She*, which Linda relaunched successfully to aim at women who were juggling the demands of career and children. Many of us are in exactly that position and we work well together, agreeing to pack everything into the daytime, with no breakfast meetings or late-nights unless it's essential. Before children, it was easy to stay late or hang around together at the end of the day; now we simply use our time more efficiently.

I have always felt that Linda and I were destined to work together. In 1976, as an ambitious Oxford graduate trying to break into journalism, I went to see a young features assistant on *Cosmopolitan* who commissioned me to write a couple of articles for her. This was Linda. I moved into book publishing and worked as an editor until 1984, when I applied for a job advertised in the *Guardian* for literary editor of *Cosmopolitan*, which in those days regularly published short stories and novel extracts. By then Linda had become deputy editor of the magazine, soon to be promoted to editor. That was when our association began, and it grew into a friendship as well.

Since we both live in North London, Linda often gives me a lift part of the way home, to Camden Town; then I catch the bus back to Kentish Town, where I have lived for ten years. Sitting in traffic jams in Portland Place and Albany Place, as Camden Council or London Electricity or British Telecom dig up the roads yet again, we have had many hours over the years to talk about things there is never time to discuss at work – our opinions of various colleagues, gossip about journalists we know and, most of all, our families, an endless source of interest. We both know that when people talk about their families, you only have to probe a little to find them riveting. Then you become involved and want to know how they are all getting on, so you need to catch up on these real-life soap operas every now and again to discover what is happening to the plot.

Linda knows a lot about my large and complicated family. She has seen me through good and bad periods, and I have always trusted her to be discreet. It is Linda, rather than any of my close friends outside work. in whom I confided one particular secret that has been worrying me for exactly four years. She knows that my brother John is HIV-positive, and that at some point he will start getting ill as his immune system is slowly depressed by the virus. Now that time has come.

When Linda sees me hunched up at my desk with my head in my hands, she comes over. Her sympathetic enquiry immediately makes me lose control and I let out embarrassingly loud sobs which I try to smother with my hands. I hope that no one else in the office is aware of what's happening, since I always like to appear self-controlled.

'It's begun,' I whisper. 'John's in the Middlesex, and it's begun.'

Linda places a hand on my shoulder and I shudder. 'I'm going to lose another bloody brother! I don't know if I can go through this again.'

'I think you should go home and find out what's happening,' she says. 'Take the rest of the afternoon off.'

As I gather up my bag and put on my coat to leave, Dick phones to tell me the same news; Adam had telephoned him earlier. I am glad not to have to go home to tell anyone, and relieved that Dick knows already, as I am afraid of breaking down in front of the children. I want to talk to them about the situation slowly and gently, without frightening them.

On the tube home my thoughts are all over the place. I keep thinking that John is going to die. I try to visualise him in the hospital and wonder what state he's in. Then I wonder how much time we have, and I can't imagine what the next few weeks or months will be like. All certainty has disappeared. How can we plan anything? I have already booked our holiday in France for August, and our magnificent trip to Thailand is scheduled for November. Will we be able to enjoy either of these? Will my brother be dead by then?

I catch myself thinking these thoughts and feel selfish. John is about to die and here I am worrying about my holidays.

While John's homosexuality is no secret in the family, few people are aware of his HIV status. No one knows except my parents, Adam, and Dick and me. For various reasons, our brother Mark and sister Jane have not been told.

I come home to a grave-faced Dick. There's nothing to be said between us. We have both known that this moment would come one day.

I want to tell the children straight away. Delay always makes revelation harder. I am in control, and I am not going to cry . . . not yet. I know that once I start to talk to them, it won't be difficult to explain.

Rebecca and Alice are not afraid to ask questions. They can tell from my face that I am being serious when I begin to talk about their uncle being ill.

'Is he going to die?' Rebecca asks immediately.

'Yes, he is,' I say. 'Not necessarily right now, but he will die fairly soon.'

'But when?' She is persistent.

I shrug. 'I don't know, but probably he won't be alive next Christmas,' I say quietly.

Rebecca and Alice turn away, hiding their faces. In silence, they disappear to their rooms. Moments later I can hear them sobbing quietly.

I telephone Jacques Azagury in the house in Islington which he still owns jointly with John, although it is now about five years since they split up. Jacques says that I should visit John the next day. He seems worried, but says that the doctors think John got there just in time.

Later, Rebecca and Alice emerge from their rooms subdued and red-eyed. I wonder whether I should have told them sooner, before the secret was officially out, but I think I have done the right thing. I explain to them that some people in the family don't yet know that John is ill, but it won't be long before they do. I quietly advise them not to talk about John at school, since some people might be horrible to them simply because they know someone with this awful disease.

The looks on their faces show that they understand they should keep silent even if they don't know exactly why. I just hope that they won't say anything prematurely to Mark and Clare.

That night I fall asleep immediately, but wake in the early hours with the memory of yesterday's news haunting me. For a brief moment I struggle to break away from the nightmare, but then realise that it is not a dream – and it is not going to go away.

Later that day at work I can hardly concentrate. I fill Linda in and tell her that I do not know what is likely to happen.

'You must just do what you have to do,' she says. At this point there are no doubts or questions.

In my lunch hour, I go to Waterstones in Charing Cross Road and start to look for books about AIDS. This is a habit; whenever anything goes wrong, I always find myself shooting off to a bookshop or library to find out as much as possible, in order to protect myself in some way. Ever since John told me he had HIV, I had read every newspaper article on the subject. Now I need to know more, to read more deeply, to read books written by specialists, not journalists.

There are a few books about AIDS. I pull one out and leaf through it for a moment, then I realise that I feel self-conscious holding it. I'm cross with myself. John's illness is not something to be ashamed of or to hide.

I flick through the book quickly to find a reference to PCP and discover that it is a form of pneumonia caused by a parasite called *pneumocystis carinii*, which commonly causes lung infection and pneumonia in people with HIV. PCP is the most frequent serious opportunistic infection for people with HIV; it can be an AIDS-defining illness. The good news is that treatment (mostly intravenous antibiotics) is most successful when started relatively early.

For the rest of the afternoon, I am very tense and I realise how anxious I am about seeing John after work that evening. I am afraid of entering the AIDS ward, of what John will look like, of how other patients will seem. Most of all, I am anxious about how I may react.

With Linda's permission, I leave early and walk up towards the Middlesex Hospital in Mortimer Street, only minutes away from my office. I want to take something to John, just a small present, but I cannot think what would be appropriate. Passing a newsagent, I suddenly know and I buy an enormous bar of Galaxy chocolate. John loves chocolate, and eats plenty of it even though he always claims it brings him out in spots.

At the hospital, I find the Charles Bell Ward on the first floor up the stairs near the chapel. As I walk in, I find myself staring at a skeleton head. I look again and see that it is, in fact, a young man. Sitting up in bed, his head looks too big for his neck. His eyes are staring. He is so thin that he looks like a Belsen victim. Is this what John will come to look like?

A male nurse approaches me and asks who I have come to see. He enquires who I am, and when I tell them I am John Dally's sister he visibly relaxes and directs me to John's bed.

I am expecting John to look terrible but, to my relief, he appears relatively well. He is lying flat. Though thinner than when I last saw him and weak and sleepy from medication, he seems muscular and solid compared with some of the other patients. The man next to him looks like the skeletal young man I have just seen on my way in.

I hand John his chocolate bar, which he seems pleased to have. I am conscious that I have not bent down to kiss him and worry that he has noticed this. But now it's too late. The moment has passed.

His eyes fill with tears every now and then, but my brother seems relatively robust and relaxed; my panic about him dying imminently subsides. 'I hope to be out by Christmas,' he says. His voice is weak.

So the doctors cannot regard this PCP as the very end, if they talk about discharging him. My spirits are lifted by the talk of life after the hospital and I feel embarrassed by my earlier panic. Was I over-reacting? Should I be calm about it all?

John sighs wearily. 'Do I look like the other people in the ward?'

I shake my head. 'You don't look anything like them,' I say reassuringly.

As John smiles, relieved, I realise how much further down the line he has to go before he dies. It is a relief but also a daunting thought.

I am struck how vulnerable he looks. It must be years since I last saw him wearing pyjamas. There is a family story about this. When he was a young child, my mother bought both him and our father new pyjamas from Marks & Spencer. Apart from the sizes, they were identical, but six-year-old John looked at Peter's six-foot-two frame and said, sternly, 'Mind you wear your own!'

I sit beside John's bed for a while and look around me, taking in the atmosphere. There is something different about the AIDS ward, which feels particularly warm and friendly. All nursing staff are dedicated but these people, who are mainly pleasant-looking males in everyday clothes, seem especially caring. I watch them talking cheerfully to the patients. One of them brings me a cup of tea. I know how hard they work, how badly they are paid, and I feel humbled by their dedication and professionalism. My own job as deputy editor of a woman's magazine seems so frivolous in the face of all this.

The Charles Bell Ward provides a wall of security for those who face hostility outside. When I comment on the notices about telephone messages and procedures, John tells me that they are very strict about any form of contact with the outside world. He had to give them a list of people he is happy to talk to on the telephone and those he does not want to speak to. This is clearly aimed at preventing the newspapers from ringing up to discover if a famous person has been admitted, but also at any family members or friends who might upset patients. Now I understand why I was approached by the nurse when I first entered the ward.

Getting up to say goodbye, I deliberately peck John on the cheek. I do feel better now but, as I leave the Charles Bell with its kind and gentle staff, I wonder how long it will be before John looks like his neighbour in the next bed with those haunting eyes, dull hair and emaciated body. Weeks or months?

Chapter Two

Growing Up in a Family of Six

Hospitals run in the family. Our parents, Peter Dally and Ann Mullins, met as students at St Thomas's Medical School in the late 1940s, where they shared a corpse called Alfred Sexton, aged 74. They married on April Fool's Day in 1950 and my brother Simon was born eleven months later, when they lived in a flat in Canonbury. Mark followed seventeen months after, then I arrived on St Valentine's Day 1954. By then the family home was a terraced house in Brixton, where Mark and I were born. Jane appeared in 1956 on 21 March, the first day of spring; this was while our father, Peter, was still recovering from the attack of polio that nearly killed him. It must have been a frightening year for my mother, who was herself in hospital with bronchial pneumonia when she had Jane and had also been told that Peter would never walk again. That same year we moved to a spacious Victorian house in West Dulwich, across the road from the Dulwich prep

School where all my brothers were to go, including John, before we moved away.

The medical prognosis was wrong. Peter did walk again and, in spite of severe residual paralysis, went on to have a distinguished medical career as a psychiatrist, first at St Thomas's and then at the Westminster Hospital. We children could see the calliper on his right leg and the strange adaptations in his car to enable him to drive, but we were too young and callous to be aware of what it might mean to him. We simply thought, with heartless glee, that we could always run away and escape from him when we had been naughty.

After Peter's polio, my parents went on to have two more children – John, on 6 June, VE Day 1959, and Adam on May Day 1961. Six of us in ten years, and we weren't even Catholics!

The large number of children in the family made us different from our friends, especially since our mother did not dedicate her life to looking after us but chose to work part-time as a doctor and medical journalist. When I was nine, a schoolfriend commented, 'My mother says your mother is an expert on family planning.' To this day I don't know if she was repeating an ironic comment or not.

Whatever the case, I grew up knowing that we were a sort of curiosity. This was in the 1950s and early 1960s; most of my friends came from neat families where even highly educated mothers did not work after having children. Dad earned the money, Mum cooked and sewed.

And other families could all fit into one ordinary car. My mother had the prototype of today's 'people carrier', a pug-nosed Bedford van which could seat twelve – three in the front, three in the middle and six in the far back. Over the years we had several models – first a couple of greys, then a frivolous primrose yellow with a black stripe down the side, followed by a dark green with a sporty red flash. Into these vans we would be ferried at weekends down to the village of Graffham, Sussex, where our grandparents – Oma and Opa – and Aunt Barbara lived and where, in 1962, we had our own weekend cottage, Wiblings Farm, known in the family simply as Wiblings.

If we stayed in London at weekends, our mother would take us around the streets of the City of London or to museums on Sundays – the 'Dead Zoo' (as we knew the Natural History Museum), the Science Museum, the V&A, the Geffrye Museum in Hackney, or Hampton Court. At the V&A we loved the Great Bed of Ware because we thought it was just about big enough for us all to sleep in. Given half the chance, we would have jumped on to it to find out.

The family could be – and was – divided in a number of ways: two boys (Simon and Mark), two girls (Emma and Jane), followed by two more boys (John and Adam). It could also be split into two, with the two elder boys and me, then Jane and the two younger boys. Our housekeeper had a daughter, Vanessa, who in age came exactly between John and Adam. Until they were much older, the collective noun for these younger three was 'the babies', a name they tolerated until they were almost teenagers. The family could also be divided in yet another way, between the older ones and the babies. Here Jane would find herself in one camp one day and the other camp the next.

The housekeeper was not a kind woman. No, I'll rephrase that – she was a monster. Although highly intelligent and competent at running the house, she kept us all in order by terrorising us. We were routinely walloped with hairbrushes, wooden coat-hangers, even the poker, if we were caught reading after lights-out. She threw the dog out of the window and threatened to make us follow if we did not behave. The wretched woman was particularly mean to John. She would lift him up by the head, with the palms of her hands flat against his ears, and yank him across the room by the ear. She was extremely cunning and her treatment of us was never harsh in public. Our parents did not know. We lived in a large house and we were always fighting and squabbling, so it was not unusual for someone to be in tears.

Years later, my mother is mortified by this state of affairs which only became known to her when we were adults. She had had a nanny as a child and thought that such people were either strict or not strict. It never occurred to her that they could be sadistic. With so much to cope with – all the children, her work and running the house – she just did not notice.

I assumed, as did my siblings, that it was normal for children to be treated in this way. I took my reasoning further and believed that children who did not have nannies to hit them were hit by their parents instead. I even felt lucky that we had a nanny so that my parents did not have to hit us.

We were all treated badly and believed there was nothing unusual about it. If we were not on the receiving end ourselves, we would watch someone else get it, which was warning enough to behave. We never discussed it with our parents; like most children, we thought that grown-ups always sided against children. We never talked about it among ourselves either, and we never mentioned it to our friends. It was only thirty years later, when I had children myself, that I realised it was not normal for children to be brutalised like this.

But at that time, this was just the way it was. The woman stayed with us for thirteen years and we were sad when she left – an odd admission, but we were afraid that someone else might be worse. At least with this one, we were used to the way she behaved and we knew how to react. But in that time she had done untold damage. John got the worst of it because he was the most vulnerable, and I think his low sense of self-esteem – which he covered up quite successfully much of the time – stemmed largely from the treatment he received at her hands. Once he was at school and it became clear that he was not a quick learner like the rest of us, it was easy for her to call him a dummy and stupid, which he believed.

This description makes it look as though we grew up in prison, but in spite of the housekeeper, our childhood was fun in many ways. We had the sort of freedom few children can enjoy in London today. For the older ones, learning to ride a bike in Dulwich was like passing a driving test – it opened up the world outside the house. Mark and I would go off for hours on our bikes, riding round the Sydenham Hill Estate, over to Herne Hill, up to Norwood, or simply round the block or to the library to exchange some books or, when the mood took us, to make some serious mischief.

Our own Victorian house was surrounded by half an acre of garden, so there was plenty of room for us all and we tended to play together well without the need for many friends. With a large family, if you fall out with one sibling there's always another to play with. And there were always pets. We had Rusty, the poor abused dog; we had hamsters that frequently escaped, a colony of over one hundred mice which had started with the two 'female' mice Mark and I bought from the pet shop in Herne Hill. We had colourful tropical fish and an enormous black-and-white rabbit that kept escaping and eating a neighbour's prize roses.

We were naughty, too. We would go to Dulwich Park and catch sticklebacks in glass jars dangling on the end of string, running away from the angry park-keepers like Peter Rabbit escaping from Mr McGregor. Some days, I'm ashamed to say, we would even drop rocks on to the railway line from the bridge across the road from the Dulwich Prep. In the summer we would creep over into a neighbour's garden, settle down inside the raspberry patch and gorge on the ripe fruit until we felt sick. We loved making bonfires, over which we would cook sizzling fat sausages to eat at the bottom of the garden. We ruined one weekend for our neighbours by dumping an old mattress in the fire. It was made of horsehair so the fumes weren't toxic, but they smell disgusting. There were a lot of angry complaints from people around us that weekend.

I was five when John was born. Being younger, he was a different kind of brother from the older ones I was used to. I had suggested the name John for the new baby and I could not wait to get my hands on him; he was a real baby and he was going to be mine. My mother said she was very happy to share him. No dolls for me. By the time Adam was born in 1961, I was well established in my role as little mother. My own mother always stressed that new babies were 'our' babies, and belonged to everyone. I still despised dolls because I did not need them: I had real babies to dress and bathe and play with. I loved to give them their bottles, swing them casually on my hip the way I had seen the housekeeper and my mother do it, and push the pram down the road as though I were a mother myself. I even liked to change their nappies, learn how to fold the thick white squares of towelling cloth and push the big safety-pins through the folds. In those days there was always a huge steaming pot on the kitchen stove full of boiling water and grey towelling nappies. Babies dominated the household, and I loved them.

My older brothers distanced themselves from the 'women and children'. Simon and Mark were consistent in maintaining the pecking order, keeping Jane and me in our places. It was hard to stand up against them for they were unquestionably stronger and more powerful, but I loathed being dominated and fought back as much as possible. I even once announced that I was so fed up with boys I was going to marry a girl. But John and Adam, these little brothers – they were different. They smiled toothlessly at me and sought out my company. Our relationship was not the same. With these brothers I could act out my powerful childish desire to be like my mother, and they always obliged. They laughed when I tickled them, followed me around and made me feel useful and wanted.

John was a particularly jolly baby who sat in his pram and grinned at everyone. One day when he was parked outside a shop, the shopping was stolen from the pram while John continued to beam at passers-by. Later, when he was about three, he ran into our local sweet-shop, grabbed a pink sugar pig, shouted 'Hi'! and, with a big smile on his face, disappeared into the street.

Babies and children dominated the household in other ways, too. My mother had forsaken a full-time hospital career because of her children, but she saw a few patients at home and did a great deal of medical journalism under her maiden name. She edited a journal called *Maternal and Child Care*, and had various columns in newspapers. In July 1961, she wrote an article about happiness and cleanliness in *Family Doctor* – the British Medical Association's magazine – in which she suggested that cleanliness was not necessarily the most important thing for a mother to focus on when bringing up children.

Her views were hardly revolutionary, but the reaction to this remark was extraordinary. The *Daily Express* commented: 'A family doctor who is the mother of six children shocked the medical world last night by attacking people who are *too* clean.'

'I think this cleanliness cult has gone too far,' my mother is quoted as saying: 'Dr Mullins pointed to her two-year-old son Johhny and said, 'See, he has a grubby face but he is happy.'

The hostilities escalated. The *Evening News* rallied in defence of the clean brigade, quoting my mother as saying that children should not be brought up to be too fastidious. Various famous people were asked their opinion and aired their views. One of these was 'Margaret Thatcher, MP and mother of twins'. Mrs Thatcher had been a contemporary of my mother's at Oxford, and even though she had not read the article she was happy to say that she found 'Dr Mullins' views extraordinary . . . I think the doctor may have over-stated her case a little. The twins need a good scrubbing at the end of a day – and they get it.'

Our mother's views on the subject of dirt got us on to the television news, too. I remember Richard Baker, then a young presenter, coming to our house with a film crew to interview the grubby little Dally children. In actual fact, we had baths every night without fail, but we were allowed to get as dirty as we wished during the day. I could not see what the fuss was about. Simon and Mark were away, so they filmed me holding baby Adam, on one end of our seesaw, while Jane and John sat at the other end.

When we all watched ourselves on the news the next day, there I was being interviewed. 'How often do you have a bath?' Richard Baker asked me. As I reply in a polite, clipped voice, 'Every day,' Jane's voice is heard in the background saying, 'She's smelly.'

The housekeeper's treatment of John was not the only factor that made him feel different from his siblings. It was hard for him to grow up in a family where considerable academic success was expected of everyone. We were sent to schools selected for their high academic standards. We had walls lined with books, and floors covered with piles of literary and medical journals. Both our parents wrote books in their spare time, and my mother's friends have always included as many writers as doctors. Margaret Drabble, Nina Bawden, George Mikes and Joan Aiken frequently came for drinks or supper.

At an early age it was evident that John had learning problems. When he was about five and attending the Dulwich prep, it was discovered that he had a reading age of nought. He had great difficulty learning to read and write. A lady in Dulwich Village started him off, and our Aunt Barbara (who had trained as a school-teacher) helped, teaching him with immense patience and understanding at a time when dyslexia was virtually unknown. John was assessed at King's College Hospital, and then at Great Ormond Street where he was diagnosed as having this word blindness. When we moved to Devonshire Place in Marylebone in 1968, my mother wrote to the London Educational Authority asking for help in finding a suitable school for her son. All she received was a photocopied list of the local primary schools.

Eventually John, aged nine, went to a special school in the East End called the Gatehouse, for children who did not fit into conventional schools. After his first visit there, he said, 'You know, Mummy, that's a very nice place. They know what people find difficult.'

He was not always so sanguine about his dyslexia, though. There were several physically handicapped children at the Gatehouse, at least one in every class. One day he came home from school and said, 'Mummy, am I a handicap?'

Once we had moved to Devonshire Place, our parents' work became an integral part of our lives, for the psychiatric practice dominated the house.

The first-floor drawing room was my mother's consulting room, while my father had the room next to it overlooking the pretty paved back garden. The ground floor was given over to a large waiting room and a consulting room let out to a private GP. The two secretaries, Mrs Lingham and Mrs Tomlins, sat at desks in the front hall, so they were the first ones to greet us as we returned from school each day. Often there would be a patient standing there settling a bill or arranging another appointment. Patients came in and out of the house from 8.30 in the morning until 7 o'clock at night.

For years the patients just seemed part of our lives, which was inevitable since the family lived on the three floors 'above the shop', and down in the basement which contained the housekeeper's and Adam's bedrooms. In the evenings, the practice telephones were switched through to our kitchen, which was on the third floor, and it was not uncommon to answer the phone to a desperate patient begging to speak to Dr Dally at maybe 10 p.m. We knew several of them by name because they left messages with us to pass on to our parents. We were instructed to say in a firm voice, 'Dr Dally is not available. The practice is closed until tomorrow morning.' Often, the poor patients sounded so distraught that I felt my parents were cruel not to talk to them there and then, but they had to set boundaries of some kind, I suppose.

All this taught me at an early age how very extraordinary humans can be. One of my first patient memories was of learning about transvestites.

We were driving down to Sussex; for some reason we were in Peter's car, not the Bedford van. This always seemed an endless journey. We still lived in Dulwich then and would take the A23 through Dorking and Horsham, then through Billingshurst and Petworth. It only took one and a half hours, but to an

eight-year-old child that seems endless. We children were constantly fidgeting and on the verge of squabbling, so my mother
tried to keep us amused by spotting pub signs and car colours,
and singing songs we had learned at the Forest School Camps
to which we were packed off during the summer.

As we played I-Spy, I noticed a cardboard box on the floor
under the driver's seat. I opened it up to find a delicate ash-
blond wig.

'Whose is this wig?' I asked.

My mother was driving. 'That belongs to one of Peter's
patients,' she said.

'Oh, doesn't she want it any more?' I hoped she would
immediately tell me I could have it.

'Well, he might,' my mother replied. 'Peter's looking after it
for him for a while. It's a very expensive wig,' she added, clearly
knowing what I was hoping. 'It's not a toy.'

By that time I did not care about having the wig. My acquis-
itiveness was not as strong as my curiosity. 'Him?'

My mother did not hesitate. I can remember now her expla-
nation that some men liked to dress up in women's clothing
because they enjoyed doing it.

I was deeply impressed and thought about this a lot for the
rest of the journey. It made sense, in some strange way. Girls
could wear trousers and skirts; perhaps it was not fair that boys
could not wear dresses and skirts? But still I could not quite
understand the wig. After all, girls wore trousers but they did
not want to have beards. It was all very puzzling to me.

Many patients meant that there were lots of stories. There
was the man and his wig, then the man who amputated his own
leg because he was in love with another one-legged man and he
wanted to model artificial limbs (he had practised on his finger
first). Another patient threatened to throw Peter out of the

window of a posh London hotel where he was causing havoc. Not to mention all the anorexic girls, several from my own school, and the addicted pop stars and depressed aristocrats and politicians who came early in the morning or late in the evening when I was setting off for school or returning home. There was also the titled lady whom my mother caught stealing a particularly exotic decoration from our Christmas tree.

We learned about auto-erotic asphyxiation in boys' public schools, manic depression, schizophrenia, personality disorders, inadequate personalities and gross hysterics. Wonderful words, they seemed exotic labels to have. And the drugs also sounded interesting – lithium, Largactil, Valium, Drinamyl, amphetamine sulphate.

But this was divorced from us. All these words related to the patients, not to us Dallys. Perhaps once a week, there was excitement about at least one patient who had behaved in a way to attract our attention. And always, at the end of the day, there was the ECT equipment lying on top of the fridge in the kitchen, the creepy combination of pads and wiring having been brought upstairs from one of the consulting rooms. Next to it might be the stale remains of a jam sandwich made earlier in the day for one of the anorexics to eat in front of my father during her session.

My parents worked hard and it was impossible not to see a few famous people along with the unknowns. Patients' names were never mentioned to us but it was inevitable that we took messages, overheard conversations or saw names on envelopes containing bills lying on the hall chest ready to be posted. It was not difficult to sense that our parents were a secret – and painful – part of many lives.

I was very sensitive to the private pain of these patients. Aware of the need for confidentiality, I did not mention their names outside the house. But sometimes I would see one of them on television or in the newspaper, in a public role, and be impressed that they could continue their lives when they were clearly unhappy at home. When they came to Devonshire Place, they could let their unhappiness show.

We would pass them daily on the stairs, as we were going to school and they were making their way up to see one of my parents on the first floor. I always averted my eyes, conscious of their embarrassment at being spotted on their way to the psychiatrist – and also aware of their own interest in their psychiatrist's family and private life.

Now of course, as an adult, I know that the Dally family is not immune from such tragedies. Many of those words apply to us, after all – manic depression, suicide, death, sadness and unhappiness. But in those days, we were different and I felt we were untouchable. It was 'them' and 'us'.

By the time we moved from Dulwich in 1968, I was not feeling so maternal towards my younger brothers. I was now fourteen and interested in teenage activities that took me outside the home and away from this huge and overwhelming family. John and Adam were an annoyance to me, the cool teenager. However, the pecking order remained in force. It was around this time that Mark, who was at Westminster, told me that he thought all Paulinas – girls who attended St Paul's Girls' School – were 'pseud'. I had to look up the word to find out what he meant. It is a difficult word to locate in a dictionary, and it took a while.

In 1969, my parents divorced. My grandfather, my mother's father, had been very disapproving of divorce and boasted that this had never happened in his family. When he died in 1968, it cleared the way for my mother to initiate proceedings. My parents had managed to keep most of the friction between them hidden from us children. I was aware of some arguments and sensitive to my mother's unhappiness at the time, and for many years I thought my father had no choice but to work at the hospital until midnight each night.

In spite of this, the tension between my parents never seemed a threat to me and I did not worry about their divorcing because I never saw us as a family in the traditional way. My fourteenth birthday in 1968, before we moved to Devonshire Place, stands out in my memory because on that occasion we all went out together as a family, to a special Chinese banquet in South London. For once everyone was there, including Peter.

Even after my parents divorced, they continued to work together in the private psychiatric practice in Devonshire Place. Peter still lived in the house. He moved into the spare bedroom, but for a while he and my mother continued to eat together in the evenings. Finally, when the housekeeper left in 1973, Peter moved down to the vacated basement flat, then into the newly available mews flat at the end of the garden where he stayed until the house was sold twenty years later. Their marriage did not work out, but they remained business partners and on speaking terms.

In retrospect, this peculiar divorce arrangement seems typical of the way my family did things. Several girls at my school had divorced parents, so I was not alone; but their parents hated each other and the children were passed from one to the other at weekends and holidays. No one had heard of a friendly divorce where the parents saw each other every day and the children stayed put. The arrangement reinforced the curiosity value of the Dally family in the eyes of our friends. And even now when I tell people about it, I can often see their astonishment. Of course, to my siblings and me it was the most natural thing in the world. Just like the dreaded housekeeper.

Few of my parents' patients knew that the two Dr Dallys were divorced, and for several years their two youngest sons did not realise either. The only time Peter caned John and Adam was around this time, after they had let off a large fire-extinguisher on the landing. (According to Adam, it was a big dare from John; John would blame Adam if he were still alive.) Adam was so incensed by the punishment that he ran up to our mother yelling, 'I think you should divorce that pig Peter!'

John and Adam were very close as little boys and remained so all their lives. While Mark and I had zoomed around Dulwich alone on our bikes, now that the family lived in central London John and Adam used the London tube to get around. On Saturdays, they would get money from our mother for Red Rover tickets which enabled them to spend all day on the underground, getting on and off wherever they wanted. Their goal was to visit every tube station on the map but they invariably got diverted, often stopping off at Victoria Station where the cartoon cinema showed films on a continuous loop. Adam was proud to have gone all the way round on the Circle Line several times, and at the age of ten was planning a career as a guard on the London Underground.

Devonshire Place is a few blocks from Madame Tussaud's and it was not long before John and Adam had discovered the back entrance. In fact, they were not interested in the wax-works; it was the amusement arcade (now defunct) that attracted them. Nonetheless, they were proud of their secret, free route into the building and were astonished when a friend of our mother, a visitor from America in his fifties, said he would prefer to go in through the front and pay rather than slip in at the back with them.

I was always critical of the way the younger boys did not seem to learn the value of money, as the rest of us had done. When we older children were growing up, our parents were just starting out on their medical careers and we lived frugally. The clothes we wore were handed down from child to child or sent over in a parcel by our wealthy American cousins. We were so scruffy that Oma used to keep a set of 'smart' clothes down in Sussex for Jane and me to wear when we stayed with her, which we were not allowed to take home to London.

Our pocket money was calculated strictly according to our age, and even though we longed for them we did not automatically expect to be given ice creams or other treats when our mother took us all off on an outing together.

By the time we had moved to Devonshire Place, our parents had progressed professionally, there was more money available and – like many younger siblings – John and Adam benefited from having older, more affluent parents who were relaxed about giving them whatever they wanted. As a teenager, it seemed to me unfair that John and Adam never had to go through the 'thrifty' years like the rest of us. I am convinced that this relative affluence at such a young age influenced the way they viewed money and material things when they were adult.

When he was thirteen John was sent as a boarder to Seaford College, up the road from Graffham, our village in Sussex. Although he hated it, the College did have a special unit for children with dyslexia. The rest of us all got into the schools my mother had chosen. Simon went first to Winchester, then Dulwich College; Mark to Westminster, then William Ellis. I went to St Paul's Girls, Jane to Mary Datchelor and then Frances Holland. Our mother did not know what was right for a child like John, and she worried constantly about his education and how he would eventually earn a living.

In 1972 my mother met Philip Egerton, a management consultant who was later to become our stepfather. Philip's own daughters were at St Christopher's, a progressive Quaker school in Letchworth, and he suggested that John and Adam be sent there. My mother – always concerned about John – was happy to try it, and he and Adam went there in 1974.

St Christopher's proved to be enough of a success for John to enjoy the rest of his school years. He and Adam also made some very good friends there, people who would remain friends long after they had all left. One of these was Imogen Bloor, the head girl, who went on to read medicine and become a GP. She always played an important part in John's life and, as it turned out, was to play a crucial part in his death.

Everyone liked Imogen. She and John were always close friends. Before I realised that John was gay, I could not understand why he did not go out with her. She was such a wonderful person, sensible, funny and clever. It would have been lovely to have her as a sister-in-law.

Another lifelong friend was Paul Chauveau, who would also be a major presence during John's last year.

At St Chris, a somewhat spartan establishment, much of the pupils' energy went into efforts to make their lives more comfortable: pinching the school TV to install in their bedrooms, for instance, or, on one notorious occasion, raiding the tuckshop. As it was a progressive school, it must have made it all the more challenging to be a rebel; naughty pranks had to be particularly impressive. Throughout his life, John fancied himself as the source of 'Big Ideas' and he came up with a few while at St Chris.

The school tuckshop supplied sweets and biscuits to the three hundred or so pupils. John's group of friends already had a forbidden key to the shop, which they would use to top up their personal supplies when needed. One day he decided that they should simply clean out the entire tuckshop and stash everything in the school dark-room, to which he also had a key: John was one of the few pupils to take a keen interest in photography during this period. Overnight they managed to move all the stock.

The next morning there was a furore when the teachers announced that all the tuck had been stolen. It took them all day to work out which other room in the school was large enough to contain hundreds of boxes of Mars Bars and Twixes, chocolate biscuits, nuts and dried fruit. But in the end, the stash was found. Since John was not the only person with the dark-room key, the crime could not be pinned on him with certainty, but the teachers seemed to have a pretty good idea. The scam also backfired when no one was allowed any tuck whatsoever that weekend, which created some bad feeling towards John and his 'Big Idea.'

At a strictly vegetarian school, many of the pupils' efforts involved getting a more varied diet and John and his friends tried to outdo each other with more ingenious pranks. One notable escapade was to nip out of the school at night and add to the notes left for the milkman by the inhabitants of Letchworth. They usually ordered cream or butter, got up early to collect the extra items before the householders opened their front doors and thus were the only ones to have cream on their breakfast cereal. They became cocky and increasingly ambitious, adding bread, bacon and sausages to the lists; this food they would bring back to cook in the small kitchenette, serving their friends an English breakfast – for a fee. They were finally found out when they added a chicken to somebody's order.

Paul Chauveau remembers John as a fifteen-year-old newcomer who rather stood out in this progressive mixed establishment, having just come from an all-boys school. He and John became best friends after a fight in which Paul broke John's nose and John gave Paul a black eye. The fight was over a girl John was interested in, and he accused Paul of trying to steal her.

'It was like a proper duel, with seconds to hold our jackets,' says Paul. The games master said to him the next day, 'I assume it was you and John Dally who put that blood all over the gym yesterday?'

From then on John and Paul were the best of friends. They were constantly fighting and arguing, but that was an integral part of an extraordinarily close relationship. Paul recalls John as always laughing and thinking up schemes. Because John found reading difficult and did not read books in his spare time, he was forever up to mischief, always plotting and planning: 'There was a constant stream of pranks from him.'

In fact, John had shown ingenuity from an early age. When he was only about seven or eight, he invented a clever device with pulleys and wooden rails for bringing the coal up the steep stairs from the coal-cellar in our house in Dulwich. For a while at school, he and Paul were sleeping in an outbuilding away from the main house, where the headmaster had placed an alarm bell in such a position that the boys had to get out of bed to turn it off in the morning. John rigged up an extension so that he could turn the alarm bell off from his bed and thus get a few more minutes' snoozing before having to get up.

A keen sportsman himself, Paul was also struck by how John had no competitive spirit in him whatsoever: 'He was such a lazy sportsman. During games, all he wanted to do was smoke cigarettes in the bushes.' But John was always tall for his age. In spite of his laziness as an athlete, at the Gatehouse he had won all the sports prizes simply because he was taller than

anyone else. And he annoyed us siblings in the country when he
volunteered to put up a mirror on the bathroom wall. At six feet
three, he was a good ten inches taller than I was and a foot taller
than Jane. He simply placed the mirror where he could admire
his handsome features, leaving the rest of us to stand on a chair
or to jump in the air if we wanted to see our own faces.

Paul recalls John as being much bigger physically than
everybody else. 'He also seemed more mature than we were
because he had several much older siblings. He had a real bank
account when we all just had post office accounts or fake
chequebooks from the St Chris "Bank".'

John's friends may have been impressed that John had been
given a bank account, but my mother was not. 'I don't know
what the bank thinks it's doing, giving a fifteen-year-old an
account of his own,' she commented one day when someone
found John's new bank card lying on the path in the woods in
Sussex, where it had lain for some months. John, of course –
already renowned in the family for his carelessness – had not
even noticed it was lost.

When they were sixteen, Paul and John bicycled around
Ireland together, starting off in Dublin where they stayed with
Paul's grandfather. They had everything they needed on their
bikes – tents, sleeping bags, fishing and crabbing tackle, calor-
gas stove. They bicycled to Galway, Limerick and finally to
Cork, camping and hanging out together.

One of Paul's memories of that trip highlights John's love of
risk-taking. Paul's grandfather enjoyed watching the racing on
television and John asked him which horse was going to win
the next race: 'My grandfather told him with some confidence
that a particular horse would win. Then John disappeared for
a while and returned, having gone down to the betting shop
and put all our money on that horse. Luckily, it won.'

For a few years Paul and John saw less of each other. John left school after 'O' Levels to do 'A' Levels at Kingsway College in London, while Paul stayed on to do his 'A' Levels at St Chris and then spent a year in the Army before going to the London School of Economics.

In 1979, just before Paul went into the Army, he and John joined up again to go on a driving holiday in France in my parents' old blue Mini. 'We had been fooling around chasing girls,' Paul recalls, 'but one evening John suddenly said, "You know, I'm gay." Then he laughed and said with a big grin on his face, "Only joking!" We were always teasing each other, so it was often hard to tell when he was being serious. I believed him; I thought he was just joking. He told me years later that the expression on my face made him realise that it was not the time to tell me. I mean, I was about to go into the Army and was pretty homophobic.'

It was around this time that John left Kingsway College, without any 'A' Levels, and our brother Mark was wondering what to do. Mark wanted to start a business and, since they were both keen on motor-bikes, he decided to launch a courier company and John joined him. Together, they started up Diplomat Dispatch. Using family contacts, they gradually built up the business, riding the motor-bikes themselves, as did their friends (including Paul, when he was at the LSE and keen to earn some extra money).

The business struggled along, competing with many other small courier companies like theirs. Then one day Mark skidded on the wet road and smashed his leg between his motor-bike and an oncoming car. He was to have numerous operations and spend many months in St Bartholomew's Hospital. It was obvious that even when he recovered, he could not ride a bike again, and he now wanted to go into the wine trade.

John continued to run the company himself and then sold it to another entrepreneur named Ken, who gave him the money to buy out Mark's share. Ken then employed John to run the burgeoning business. When Adam left school, he wanted to earn money straight away rather than go on to university and so, after a long stay in Australia, he joined John in 1980.

I never met Ken, but he sounded an interesting character. A working-class man who built up an empire of courier companies, he developed expensive tastes and spent his money on fancy restaurants, flashy cars, works of art and trips to the opera. When John told me he went to the opera with Ken, I thought it a bit odd. 'Do you think Ken's homosexual?' my mother asked me one day. I conceded that Ken probably was, but I was adamant to my mother that John was not. It did not occur to me even then that he might be.

By now it was 1981 and I was living in New York with Dick. We first met in London, in 1976, when I began working as an editor in a small American publishing company where Dick was editor-in-chief. In 1980, the firm went bankrupt and I was made redundant. Dick had already left to embark on a writing career and we decided to live and work in New York (where Dick originally came from). We were extremely poor and earned what we could from freelance editing and writing. In the hot summer months, we took our work and typewriters up to Vermont where Dick's parents had a house in the hills. John came out to visit us, having arrived in New York to visit friends who in the event proved unwelcoming. He seemed anxious to get out of the city, which he found claustrophobic, and we met him off the train at White River Junction.

This was the first time I was aware of John's growing affluence; he insisted on buying three lobsters and a bottle of champagne for our supper. He spent two nights with us before returning to New York; we played 'Risk', went fishing for trout in the nearby Waites River and talked late into the night discussing the family.

I was sorry to say goodbye to him. It was the first time that I had seen John as an adult rather than my little brother, and I liked him.

A few months later, we heard terrible news from London. Ken was not only homosexual, but it seemed, enjoyed the rough stuff. One night he was found murdered by a rent boy he had picked up that evening. He died a horrible, violent death, which left all his staff in shock and the business in disarray.

With Ken gone, John and Adam continued to run the company, now called A-Z Couriers, but found themselves embroiled in a battle involving Ken's sister Betty – who had inherited her brother's estate – and Ken's old office manager, John Lander, who wanted control of the business. In 1983, there was a brief power struggle and various lawsuits. John and Adam settled with Betty for £35,000, leaving them with the business. Then they managed successfully to sue John Lander for exactly £35,000 for breach of an undertaking he had made to the court concerning their case.

The boys were rolling in money by this time. They loved a fight, particularly if they won. John bought himself a large silver Mercedes and then, with sadistic relish, he had John Lander pay off his debt of £35,000 in monthly cheques made out to the A-Z Number Two Motoring Account.

The boys were the archetypal 1980s success story. They were featured in *Cosmo Man*, a supplement developed by the main magazine; they were runners-up in the Young Entrepreneur Competition run by the *Independent* newspaper. They spent money like crazy – if they wanted something, they bought it immediately. At the age of twenty-four John was driving his silver Mercedes, taking five-star holidays in exotic places and spending money as though it would always be there. They thought they were geniuses. 'The more money we were making,' Adam says now, 'the greater the debt. We figured the party would go on for ever. We never stopped to think how it was that we had got into this position. We thought it was us. Everything we touched seemed to turn to gold. It was crazy. We lived like rock stars, only without the cocaine.'

During this time they ate out at all the fancy restaurants. They were thrown out of Nico Landenis' restaurant in Clapham, after they had ordered gin and tonics and moved the chairs around (their story, but I'm sure there was more to it), and on one occasion they went to La Gavroche where they ordered Harvey Wallbangers as cocktails and got the giggles. John ordered the famous Gavroche duck with liver and then sent it back because he had not realised that it contained liver.

Adam bought himself a pedigree Dalmatian puppy which he named Pimms. Pimms was only a few months old when she caught and killed two of Oma's fancy chickens. Anxious to appease his angry grandmother, Adam immediately tracked down the breeder of these special chickens and bought two pullets to replace the dead ones. He and John arrived at Wiblings one Friday evening with the box containing the birds, which they placed on the lawn. Typically, and without thinking, John casually opened the lid to see how the chickens were. The birds shot out of the box and landed on the grass. Pimms instantly pounced on one and killed it, while the other flapped across the lawn and disappeared into the hedge. Oma had to wait another week before her chickens were finally replaced.

John was exceptionally generous with his money, paying for others, buying expensive presents and taking people out to dinner. Whenever he took Dick and me out for a meal – which he always did on our visits over here from New York – he invariably paid the taxi driver in advance to take us home.

Dick and I always appreciated his generosity. In the early 1980s we still had very little money. We had now returned to live in London, where Dick was writing a book and I was eking out a living as a freelance book editor. Even when I got myself a full-time job as literary editor of *Cosmopolitan* in 1984, money was still tight. But it made me uneasy to see my little brother spending so much and so freely. I was, of course, happy to eat caviar at the Savoy with him, but deep down I did feel slight disapproval of this extravagance. Perhaps it was simply envy, but I knew I would rather do my job on *Cosmo* for an okay salary than run a courier company for a fortune.

John was to feel it too. At the age of twenty-five, he became so bored with work that he did not know what to do with himself and even talked about retiring.

Our mother was so alarmed at John's plans that she suggested he travel the world a bit more – perhaps go somewhere like Australia for a while. John jumped at the idea and made plans with his usual fiscal abandon. Just before leaving, he took the entire family – including uncles, aunts and cousins – to dinner at the Connaught before he set off across the world. (He was to return a year later, unknowingly infected with HIV.)

The younger boys' financial success visibly bothered Simon, the eldest in the family. Simon had had a promising career in book publishing, and was an extremely learned chap. He had read English at Oxford, was witty and clever, spoke three languages and was passionate about Italian art. In our family he was closer to the norm than John and Adam. But the older he became, the more envious he was of his younger brothers' success. It was as if he felt they had no right to surpass him, the eldest. The pecking order remained.

Simon had started his career as an editor at Weidenfeld & Nicolson, the book publishers. He soon had his own sports list and enjoyed life, with many friends and colleagues. He was happily attached to Ann Wilson, another editor at Weidenfeld's, who was welcomed into the family and well liked. To me, she became like a big sister.

Then he began to change. He did not like the rest of us finding partners and moving away from the family. He despised marriage and the idea of procreating. From being the older brother I was proud of, he became an embarrassment. He was forever scheming and plotting, and lost his job at Weidenfeld's for serious disloyal behaviour. By now it was obvious that he had a severe drinking problem and had lost all sense of how others saw him. He got other publishing jobs, but his heart was going out of books. Then he became obsessed with computers and increasingly isolated from his large number of friends, closeting himself away in his Clapham flat and seeing few people apart from John and Adam, as if he felt that they at least respected him. The relationship with Ann Wilson ended, though they remained good friends, isolating him from his peers all the more.

Determined to make money as an entrepreneur as well, he left book publishing in 1984 to set up his own computer game company which he ran from the offices of A-Z. He seemed obsessed with wealth. The three brothers became quite close-knit and secretive. But they did make it known that they had rewritten their wills to leave everything to each other to protect the company, and they had all taken out huge life insurance policies. They were all so young and had no dependants. I remember thinking how weird it was that they had so much money and they took out insurance policies they did not really need. Those were the days of greed.

I still did not know that John was homosexual and, looking back now, I see how dense I was. I always thought it strange that although he clearly attracted girls, he never had serious girlfriends. I put it down to his being intellectually insecure – never able to find someone the family approved of – and too much of a perfectionist to find a woman suitable for him. Even when the outward signs were there I was blind to them. I blush now when I remember wondering why he chose to dress in the gay uniform of tight white T-shirts, jogging bottoms and trainers, with his hair cut short. 'Why does he dress as if he's gay?' I used to wonder. It amazes me now. I had just spent three years living in New York and was perfectly at ease with openly gay men. Yet I was incapable of standing back sufficiently to recognise it in my own brother. It was Adam who finally told me what was what in 1984. Once he did, I could see that it was obvious to anyone who had their eyes open, and had been for years.

As I said, this was in the early 1980s, after Dick and I had spent three years living in New York. It was during the time we were there that the first reports about a strange disease – which seemed at that stage to affect only gay men – were coming out in the American press. Right-wingers would gleefully describe it as God's punishment to sodomites for their deviant ways.

One summer weekend in 1982, Dick and I went to stay with a friend of Dick's in his family house in upstate New York. Various other friends came over that day, one of whom was gay. As we sat by the lake in the baking sun and drank our beer, there was a lot of talk of this frightening and peculiar disease which appeared to be getting more common by the week. One or two knew of people who were afflicted by the illness, but very little was known about it then. It was identified as Kaposi's sarcoma in those days, a rare skin cancer previously only seen in

Jews. I was interested in the mystery of it and concerned about our gay friends. It would be a long time before I thought I needed to worry about it within my own family. But now, two years later, a few words from Adam turned what had been a possible threat to friends into a threat to my own sibling. I worried whether John was careful.

It was in 1984, after he had come back from Australia, that John came out as a homosexual. By now he was an extremely rich young man and he was feeling very confident about himself. He was doing well and felt secure. And now he told Paul the truth – without claiming it was a joke.

'I realised that he meant it when he brought a boyfriend back home for the night one time,' says Paul. He also realised that since John was his best friend, he would have to accept his sexuality. 'There I was, an Army officer and a rugby player, and my best friend was gay. I think I went overboard to prove that I accepted him as he was. John decided he was going to show me the gay scene. Pretty soon, at one gay club, I bumped into someone I knew from the LSE.'

Since casual sex was the greatest threat to John, I was immensely relieved when he settled down in a relationship with Jacques Azagury, a fashion designer.

We all loved Jacques. He too was one of six, a French-Moroccan-Jewish family that had come to England in the early 1960s. Jacques fitted into our family easily. He and John bought a beautiful flat in Highbury, where they lived in some style. Jacques has exquisite taste, and everything in the flat always looked perfect. He also advised John on how to dress, and his taste became John's taste. My brother seemed to need Jacques to give him an image of some sort. He had no confidence in his own instincts except about business, but what he did have was his sexuality and his good looks. Six-foot-three-inches tall, with a strong athletic body, John looked like a young James Hunt, the then racing driver. Attractive to either sex, he was blond and handsome, sweet and charming, also of course extremely rich and generous. For Jacques, who was five feet four and, for all his fame and success as a designer, did not seem to make vast sums of money, John was a definite catch.

Jacques was fun and funny, and because of my work in the magazine world I always felt I could talk with him easily. Dick was also fond of him and for many years we invited them to our annual Thanksgiving dinner.

Then everything started to go wrong. John and Adam's early success had made them think that life would always be good to them, and they had no experience of bad trading conditions. In 1988 they over-expanded and were unable to borrow more from the banks when they needed it. They turned to my mother, who lent them some money which they repaid promptly. They borrowed again, but this time they were not able to repay it as they had promised. It transpired later that my mother had allowed them to use Wiblings, the country house, as collateral. The bank would hold the deeds to the house for many years.

This arrangement caused a lot of annoyance in the family. There was genuine concern that they might never pay back the money and my mother would lose Wiblings. There was also annoyance with her for being so naïve about the boys' business acumen. It was obvious to the rest of us that they were getting out of their depth but incapable of changing their way of life. They still lived grandly, as if they had to get through this bad period without anyone noticing.

In early 1989 John and Jacques moved to an early Victorian property in Alwyne Road, Canonbury. John saw the house and loved it; he wanted it and had to have it even though it was a foolish purchase. It was a beautiful residence, but it had a very short lease on it and was greatly over-priced. He and Jacques mortgaged themselves to the hilt to buy it. Perhaps John did not care that the lease had only 30 years to run. Perhaps he did not even think about that. But it was typical of him to act on impulse without considering the implications. I later discovered that it was around this time that he and Jacques stopped being a sexual couple. They remained friends but saw other people – rather like my own parents.

Elsewhere in the family, there were other problems. Simon had been behaving oddly for some years now, and in the autumn of 1988 he was diagnosed as having manic depression. This was after he had stolen a large number of priceless antiquarian books from a private collection, planning to stash them away as his 'pension'. The crazy plan went wrong and Simon was caught and arrested. He was out on bail, with his case due to come up later in the spring of 1989. It was likely that his illness would have made the court treat him gently, but Simon was ashamed of what he had done and very frightened of this illness and what it meant. He could face the world no longer.

The future was bleak. Simon also suffered from severe psoriasis and this condition, we were told, meant that he could not take lithium – which stabilises most manic-depressives – because it would exacerbate the skin disease.

My parents got him referred to a psychiatrist, but although Simon liked him, the man seemed completely ineffectual. Simon's situation appeared hopeless.

On Good Friday 1989, a few weeks before his court case, he came down in the car to Wiblings with Dick and me and our girls.

Simon died on Easter Sunday. All of us except Jane were there. We had had an Easter-egg hunt for the children in the morning, then a family lunch which included my grandmother and aunt. In the afternoon, Adam and John returned to London and Dick and I took Rebecca and Alice up the road to visit my grandmother for tea. She chose to be called Oma (which means 'Granny' in German) when Simon was born, since she was only forty-eight and did not wish to be called 'Granny'. She was a weaver and had been awarded an OBE for her contribution to the craft world. Although she no longer had the strength to use the beater on the loom very much, she still made wonderful pile rugs.

Oma had just finished making a rug for Alice, although it was much smaller than the one she had made for Rebecca two years earlier. At eighty-four, she had less energy; age was catching up with her. However, she was still alert and relatively active. My mother was planning to hold a birthday party for her eighty-fifth birthday in two weeks' time. No one knew at that moment that the occasion would be changed from an old lady's birthday party to a young man's wake.

It was a sunny day. The sky was a clear blue and the buds were coming out on the trees. It was the Equinox, and the clocks had changed that morning. It was wonderful to have it so light and to know that the long summer lay ahead. Winter was at last behind us.

It was time to get the children ready for bed, so we said goodbye to Oma and walked down the road. I was pushing Alice in the buggy while three-year-old Rebecca held Dick's hand. Our world was about to be shattered.

As we walked in through the gates of Wiblings Farm, I saw Simon sprawled out on the lawn in front of the house. He was on his stomach, his head away from us. For a second I thought he was having a nap. 'What's Simon doing?' I said aloud. But as I spoke I saw the handle of the shotgun sticking out between his legs. He was lying on top of it. I knew about that method; somewhere I had read about killing yourself that way. You lie on the gun and stick the end of the barrel in your mouth. Lying on it stops the kickback throwing you backwards and jerking the gun from your hands. I knew he was dead. He was thirty-eight.

Dick walked over to him, then came back to us quickly. 'He's done it. Take the children indoors,' he said. 'You have to tell your mother.'

Simon had shot himself. We knew he was depressed and that suicide was a possibility but we had not expected it.

I ushered the children past Simon and into the house. I could see my mother sitting out on the terrace in the back garden with Mark and Clare; Clare was heavily pregnant with her first child. I handed the children over to Dick and took a deep breath, then I walked up the slope towards the group. 'Something's happened,' I said. My voice sounded so feeble.

'Simon's done something to himself.' I could not get the words out, though I don't usually use euphemisms.

Seeing the look on my face, my mother rose to her feet. 'He's shot himself,' I said.

Mark and Mum started to run into the house. 'It's too late,' I called, but they had disappeared. I spun round to a horrified Clare. 'It's too late, he's dead!' My voice cracked and I found myself crumbling to the ground.

The rest of that day remains only as fragments of memory in my head. Simon lying on the lawn as the evening sun went down. The black van and the long wooden box they put him in to take him to the morgue. Peter and his friend Anne Norwich driving over from Peter's house five miles away, white-faced with shock. Most of us drinking tea; Dick, the American, mixes himself a martini. The police quizzing my stepfather Philip and then Peter about what happened. Then John and Adam driving back from London having heard the news; Simon's girl-friend ringing up from London, hysterical, having just read his suicide note. Philip hosing down the lawn. Rebecca, confused, afraid to go to bed because Simon had gone to sleep on the lawn and died. The stunned silence. The sudden feeling of absence, of Simon never being there ever again.

Simon's funeral was the last time we were all together. It was a secular service in Chichester, with my uncle Edwin, an experienced TV and radio broadcaster, acting as the MC. A professional singer sang Italian songs and Simon's best friend, Alan Chance, gave a warm speech which conveyed the intelli-gent and interesting Simon we had known before he became ill. The crematorium was packed with writers and publishers Simon had worked with over the years, family and other people who knew and liked him and had not witnessed his recent dete-rioration. The food my mother had ordered for Oma's eighty-fifth birthday was now eaten at my brother's wake at Wiblings.

Simon's death was a violent shock to all of us. For weeks it felt as though we were all cut off from the world and from each other.

In the last few months of his life, he had fallen out with his younger brothers. On the day after he died, along with the sui-cide note addressed to our mother, I found an informally written will in the briefcase he had left in his bedroom at Wiblings. In it he left his estate to be divided up between his siblings, with certain amounts going to his old girlfriends.

Worried about losing control of their company, and needing the money from Simon's estate to cover their mounting debts, John and Adam were at pains to prove that the will was void. Even though the document was officially not valid, the rest of the family felt that Simon's final wishes should be honoured and were rather shocked that Adam and John did not agree with this. The boys said they would honour the unofficial will once they had sorted out their business problems, but it would be many years before this happened.

Simon's life insurance policy delivered half a million pounds to John and Adam, which was swallowed up by their business. Even that did not remedy their financial state. Their debts had spiralled out of control and soon they were in the humiliating position of having to sell the British part of the company to another courier firm, for whom they then had to work for some months.

The moment they were able to do so, they moved to New York, where the American side of the business was proving healthy. In New York their riders rode push-bikes through Manhattan's polluted streets. John and Jacques remained good friends, and Jacques still lived in the house in Alwyne Road. John would come over to London every now and then and he came to supper, sometimes with Jacques and sometimes not. At this point, I was not sure of the status of their relationship. When I rang, I would always invite them as a couple because nothing had ever been said to make me think I should act otherwise.

Simon's death and their behaviour over the will smashed whatever links there were between John and Adam and Mark and Jane. The boys kept up sporadic contact with Dick (whom they seemed to respect as a big-brother substitute), our parents and me.

We remained sufficiently in favour to be invited to a huge thirtieth birthday party which Jacques gave for John a few weeks after Simon's death, in the new A-Z offices in Islington. It was an astonishing event, which left Dick and me feeling quite old and out of it. Paul Chauveau and Imogen were there, otherwise we didn't know anyone. But it was also exhilarating and fun. I remember heaving bodies everywhere, and John being particularly excited and wild.

John's thirtieth birthday party was also memorable for being the occasion when Adam told me that he, too, was gay. I left the party shocked and reeling from the news, but with no less affection for my youngest brother than I had always had. I was surprised, but I think Adam had only recently realised it himself. My main feeling was fear of HIV infection for him, too.

On 6 November 1989, John was over from New York and I invited him and Jacques to supper. John arrived without Jacques. 'Jacques is working,' he said simply. I was not sure how they conducted their relationship across the ocean, but I knew heterosexual couples who did the same and I always felt it safer to assume that they were still together. That night, John told me otherwise and more.

He told us that he was very fond of Jacques, and that they would always remain friends; he said that Jacques had been very good to him when he was ill. He repeated this several times until it dawned on me that he was trying to tell us something. John looked anxious as I asked quietly, 'What do you mean?'

Tears flooded his eyes as he said, 'I'm HIV-positive.' Then he waited.

I could tell that he just did not know what reaction to expect. I got to my feet and went over to him. As I put my arms around him, he burst into tears. 'I've been wanting to tell you for so long,' he sobbed, 'but I just didn't dare.'

It turned out that he had known since 1986, when his doctor – also gay and destined to die of AIDS – noticed swollen lymph glands and suggested he be tested for HIV. In those days it took weeks for the test results to come back. The day John got the positive results, Adam went round to the flat to find him in floods of tears. 'We had tickets to *The Mikado* that night,' Adam recalls. 'During the interval we shared a punnet of ice cream and John himself suddenly said that he thought he should not share the wooden spoon with me. In those days we knew so little about how the virus was passed from one to another.'

Soon after that, John said, he told our mother and Peter. So our parents had known all along. John then explained that the thirtieth birthday partry Jacques had given for him a few months earlier had been particularly wild because it was celebrating the fact that John had reached the age of thirty, which he had never expected to do.

John then made us promise to keep this news a secret. 'You just never know how people will react,' he said. 'It's not just family, it's also banks and insurance companies. You can never tell what new rules they might bring in to exclude people with HIV. It could be a disaster.'

'Of course,' we said. I could see the seriousness of the situation and understood. If he had not dared tell Dick and me, whom he did trust, how could he have taken a risk with others to whom he was not so close? And why should he?

I was a little hurt that he thought that I might reject him, but I was touched too that he had not told me precisely because he valued our relationship and wanted to hang on to it for as long as possible.

The news was particularly shocking because for so long I had thought that John was in a stable relationship with Jacques. I had assumed this lessened the chances of his getting HIV. But he had caught the virus before he ever met Jacques, and Jacques is one of those rare individuals who have proved to be resistant to it. Now I knew that at some point in the fairly near future, my brother was going to die a horrible death. His famous life insurance policy for one million pounds would be paid out sooner rather than later. It was weird to think that this wondrous amount of money would be released after a tragic event. It was no longer if; it was when.

In fact, Joh's death not happen for some years.

The question of when hangs over us now on the evening in December 1993. John still looks remarkably fit. He has always been narcissistic and looked after himself fairly well. I know enough about AIDS, however, to be aware that once the immune system has been depressed below a certain level, the body is unable to stand up against all the diseases that start attacking it. Once the first serious illnesses get a hold, a battle has begun in which the virus always wins.

But now, at the age of thirty-nine, I have already lost one brother, Simon, and the impending loss of John is a certainty. From being one of six children, I had become one of five. Soon it would be four. Simon's death four years previously was sudden and shocking, but I still remember something Mark said that day as some of the policemen still combed the garden for clues while others quizzed my stepfather and then my father about what had happened. And all the time Simon's body lay stretched out on the lawn, with the evening light gradually fading into dusk. As we watched from the house, still trembling with the shock, Mark quietly said, 'I find it odd to think that I am now the eldest child.' I thought, too, how odd it was to move up a notch. Now I think that when John dies, the family will contract again and I shall have only two brothers.

So who was this third brother of mine, the second one about

to die? John's charm and smiles covered up an insecure little boy who was convinced that he was stupid. He remained attached to the family and always found hostility from older siblings very upsetting. Kind and generous, he could also be shockingly selfish and thoughtless. He was immensely loyal and caring to those he liked, and inspired great loyalty in others. Although by escaping the influence of a formal education, he felt inferior in the company of educated people, his thoughts and ideas, albeit naïve, were honest and unguarded, giving him a spontaneity of thought that could be immensely refreshing. Even though he rarely read a newspaper and never read a book, John was always engaging company, full of curiosity and interesting observations about life.

Chapter Three

December–January

A few days after the December weekend when John flies in, Oma is admitted to hospital in Chichester with pneumonia. This seems too much to bear. I suggest to the children that they make some get-well cards for her. Rebecca flies into a rage and refuses. Only four months before, Roger Toulmin, a great family friend, had died of cancer. When he first went into the hospice in Hampstead, Rebecca had made a beautiful card for him, with the message 'Get Well Soon'. But he died a few weeks later.

'Why should I write a card for Oma?' she demands now. 'I made one for Roger and it didn't work.'

Charmed by my daughter's sense of omnipotence, I remember now that after Roger had died, she was particularly worried about the fate of her card. Perhaps she thought its magic had failed, and that she had let Roger down.

Oma is out of hospital before Christmas, quite robust again. She always seems to bounce back. She still does not know about

John. Few people do; just my parents, myself and Dick, Adam – and of course Jacques. This is John's secret and he still does not want anyone else to know about it.

In the middle of December, my nephew Tom is christened at the Catholic church where Roger Toulmin's funeral was held. My parents are non-believers and we children were not christened. Nor are mine. But Mark's wife Clare is a practising Catholic and Tom, the third child, has reached his christening day.

I sit in a wooden pew in the gloomy church and wonder what the priest would say if he knew that this baby boy's uncle is dying of AIDS. I wonder what Clare's family would say too. It's just as well so few of us know at the moment. It would surely spoil this happy family occasion, just as Simon's death on Mark and Clare's wedding anniversary must always mar that day for them. I am relieved that Ruth chooses to run around the church and I have to occupy myself chasing after her.

Afterwards, the party at Mark and Clare's has a surreal quality about it, with the tiny baby dressed in a fancy white christening suit and both families there for this new little Dally boy. Clare has worked hard for the occasion – a family gathering with champagne and a huge spread of sandwiches, smoked salmon and salads.

I watch my mother across the room and wonder if her thoughts are more on the other Dally boy lying in the hospital bed than on little Tommy. We are divided into those who know and those who do not. I feel quite alienated by the whole event. It is odd to see my brother Mark, so lawless as a child, acting the part of the proud father of a baby son now safely a member of the Catholic church.

The following week Mark and Clare come to a pre-Christmas supper with some other friends. We exchange presents and drink champagne. They know nothing about John.

It is a laboured evening. My thoughts are a tangled mess and I don't talk much. It is excruciating having this secret, which they too will have to hear fairly soon. What a curse a secret is! I know that those left in the dark will be very upset when the truth does come out, and they will be angry with those who already know. The secret itself has grown more complicated too. At the moment they are unaware, as we toast each other, that John is lying ill in a bed in the Middlesex Hospital, just down the road. They think he is in New York. That is one part of the secret. The other part is the fact that they have been excluded from the knowledge of his HIV status for over four years. It's never pleasant to be left out, however good the reason for it, and I feel very shifty in their presence. But John has sworn Dick and me to secrecy, so what else can we do except smile and act like happy hosts, looking forward to the Christmas break and New Year?

John is allowed home for a few hours on Christmas Day for what Adam describes as a 'miserable Christmas at home in Alwyne Road with Jacques, David, Adam and Kenny Everett'.

For the rest of us it is a relatively small family gathering this year. Dick and I take the children down to Sussex. There we have a Christmas dinner as always, on Christmas Eve in the European tradition. My great-grandfather was a Russian German, so as a family we always open our pile of presents at drinks time on Christmas Eve before sitting down to the usual meal of turkey, roast potatoes and Brussels sprouts. Children go to bed after the drinks, if too young to stay up for dinner, or after the meal if they have joined in. But all lay out their stockings at the ends of their beds for Father Christmas to fill when they are asleep.

Our children are still too young to stay awake for the dinner, so the meal – carefully cooked by Dick – is shared only with my grandmother, Oma. My Aunt Barbara is eating with friends. Mark and Clare have taken their children to Liverpool to stay with Clare's mother. Adam is in New York, and Jane at home up in Yorkshire.

Christmas Day begins early, with the opening of the stocking presents. We are is free to lounge around playing with new toys and games or reading new books. For meals we eat cold turkey sandwiches and cold stuffing.

Since having children, the fun of Christmas has returned to me and I find myself annually recalling the festivities of my childhood. This year is all the more vivid and poignant; watching the children open their presents and squeal with delight and pleasure reminds me of my little brothers so many years before. John does not care about this Christmas and is unlikely to see another one.

The tension is almost unbearable, wanting to talk about John with my mother and Philip but unable to do so because of Oma at the table. I feel increasingly guilty at excluding my grandmother, but there's no alternative at the moment.

The next day we ring John in the hospital. At first the nurse says he is not on his bed, but soon he calls back. 'I've been in the hospital chapel,' he says. 'Did you know that hospitals all have chapels?' he asks. It is typical of John to be surprised by such a fact.

I feel a sudden uneasiness. 'What were you doing there?'

'Oh, just thinking,' he replies dreamily. He sounds remarkably calm.

I have a sudden dread that he might become religious as he approaches death. I would find that very difficult to cope with, though it would not surprise me if John suddenly embraced some faith. Since he became HIV-positive he has expressed somewhat primitive ideas about spirituality and about 'seeing the light'. He once said, in all seriousness, that he had had an experience in which he had seen and spoken to Simon. I could cope with seeing lights, but the idea of his believing in a Christian God at this stage would drive a big wedge between us. No doubt I am worrying unnecessarily. John probably just liked the peaceful atmosphere of the hospital chapel.

Mum speaks to John next and he says he would like to see Jane. Now he apparently does not care who knows about his condition and he wants Jane to be told the truth, I hope this means he is willing for other family members to be informed.

John was once very close to Jane, when the two of them used to go on holidays together in Ireland. Until they fell out over their work and Simon's will, and Jane moved up to Yorkshire, they had always been great pals. The feelings are still there, and I feel a twinge of jealousy. He sees me more as a maternal figure than as a friend. All those walks in the pram and nappy changes . . . they did their work too well.

Nevertheless, I feel a great weight has been lifted. Now, at last, we have John's permission to be open. The past few weeks have been very uncomfortable.

John is really quite cheerful. His pneumonia has gone and he expects to be discharged within days.

Afterwards, my mother says, 'Let's ring Jane.' Then she hesitates. It is clear that she does not want to say the words herself. Possibly she is afraid of breaking down – my mother who has lived through so many disasters and survived. Perhaps this is just the last straw.

Philip takes charge and telephones Jane, who is devastated by the news. For her, too, it seems that all the years of acrimony are pushed aside as her feelings for her younger brother are rekindled. All the rage about their business dealings, their borrowing against Wiblings, dissolves. She says she will come down to London to see him immediately.

Now Mum can tell Mark, too. At last the facts can all come out.

Coming back to London before New Year, I go to visit John in hospital, expecting him to be ready to leave any day. Instead, I find him in an isolation ward. Notices on the door warn visitors to put on gloves and a protective apron before entering the room.

John looks miserable. Just when he was expecting to be discharged, he was told that he has developed shigellosis, a form of dysentery and a notifiable disease. HIV patients are susceptible to every opportunistic infection going, and shigella could have a devastating effect on all John's fellow patients. As a result, he must be isolated from the main ward.

He is very gloomy. Having looked forward to escaping from the hospital, he is now trapped until further notice. He is not even allowed to use the ward telephone, though Paul has lent him his mobile phone which sits on the table beside his bed.

'I feel like a leper,' John says. But he cheers up as he tells me about a visit from Imogen. 'She's so wonderful, she's such a good friend.'

By coincidence, Imogen is John's doctor. A few years ago, she became a partner at the surgery in Islington where Jacques was already registered. Although John was living in New York at the time, when he stayed in London he was able to register at the practice because Alwyne Road was the catchment area, and thus he became one of Imogen's patients. Over the coming months, this is to be a source of great comfort to both John and the rest of the family. In fact, until he came back to London with PCP, his health was fine and he rarely needed to see Imogen for any medical reasons.

In view of the notice on John's door, I do not kiss him when I arrive. But ten minutes into my visit, Jacques arrives from work and, disregarding all the rules, bounds in and kisses John on the mouth. I watch this display of affection and smile; it is both touching and shockingly irresponsible. Jacques apparently doesn't realise that he could spread the dysentery around outside the hospital as a result of his bold, affectionate greeting.

On 28 December, I go to a party given by my friends Chris and Vicky Huhne. I have known Chris since our Oxford days, and have always enjoyed their annual festivities. Despite not being christened myself, I am also godmother to their youngest child, Peter.

Dick hates parties and rarely comes, so I am on my own today. Having left the house anxious to see people other than family, once I arrive I realise that I do not feel at all sociable. I give my godson his Christmas present, and play for a short time with his delightful elder sister Lydia. Luckily I spot my friend Debbie Postgate across the room with her husband David. I have known Debbie since we were eight. We went to the same schools, to the same college, St Hilda's, at Oxford. Debs has known my family for years and has always had a soft spot for my little brothers. I find myself telling her about John and wanting to hear what she has to say. Knowing she had a lawyer friend called Gareth, who recently died of AIDS, I quiz her relentlessly about the progression of his illness in the last years. What she tells me does not cheer me up. It is clear that there is a gruelling time ahead.

Chapter Four

January–February

John is now out of hospital and living a relatively normal existence. Life takes on a strange routine of seeing him once a week for lunch in town near my office when we are both free, and then he and Jacques come to our house for dinner every other week or so. In between I work on my novel and attend the parties and book launches that I have to go to after office hours. They sometimes seem more like a duty but I enjoy most of them, seeing colleagues and like-minded book people.

Jane has been down to see him and now keeps in touch by telephoning him regularly. The re-establishment of their friendship means a great deal to John.

But as he gets better, John grows restless. His home is now in New York, as is his work, and he wants to return to America as soon as he feels well enough but is not sure what he can do in the meantime. Since he is not a great reader and is not fit enough to pursue any sport, time hangs heavily.

I have recently done some computer training at work and we talk about the possibility of his taking a computer course. It seems to interest him; he buys an Apple Powerbook for several thousand pounds and plays around with it for a while. Then he leaves it out in the rain. This is typical of him – forgetful and casual even about precious possessions.

Being close to death does not alter one's essential nature, and in many ways John does not change at all during these horrendous months. He has always been the least academic of us six children, though severe dyslexia did not prevent him from building the successful business with Adam which – despite hiccups – still provides them with a comfortable way of life. But John retains an endearing artlessness that always triggers in me a sisterly protectiveness.

The year 1994 is one of birthdays as well as death. My grandmother is coming up to her ninetieth, and I am approaching my fortieth on 14 February, St Valentine's Day.

I am planning to have a joint fortieth party with my old friend Adam Sisman, in my parents' house in Devonshire Place. My parents are retiring and closing down their psychiatric practice, so they are selling the family house where they ran it for twenty-five years.

Our old home is a large, elegant Georgian terraced house where Nelson's mistress, Emma Hamilton, is reputed to have lived. Its grand, high-ceilinged reception rooms were built for parties like the one Adam and I are planning. It also seems an appropriate venue for Adam and me, as a goodbye to the house where we hung out together in teenage gangs at weekends when my parents and the younger children were away in the country. It houses memories of adolescent pranks and

rebellions, rows with the parents. My past feels as much a part
of it as the Adam ceilings and polished mahogany doors. It
reminds me of myself and my siblings when we all first moved
there in 1968, filling up the enormous space like water flooding
into an empty chamber.

Meanwhile, back in Kentish Town, we are feeling squeezed
in our Victorian terraced house and have decided to add a new
study for me so that seven-year-old Rebecca can take over my
present study as her own bedroom. We have employed the
services of a surveyor called Phil, who has drawn up the plans
and sorted out the planning permission. He also tells us that he
has found a good builder called Dave, whom he can recommend because he has done some work for Phil himself.

The building work is going to be very disruptive because
they will have to rip down the old Victorian back extension
and build it up again from the bottom, since it was built without foundations. Given John's state of health, I wish we could
put it all on hold, but the trouble is that we do not know how
long he is likely to live. We agree that they will begin work in
April, after Easter. We have to go ahead, even though we know
there will be months of inconvenience at a time when we least
need it.

'Having the builders in' is never exactly pleasant but, as Dick
and I make the plans and look at blueprints, fortunately we
have no idea just how awful this particular job will be.

In mid-January, John comes to Sussex in the car with us for
a weekend. Jane comes too. She has been down to London to
visit John for a day recently, but before that they had not seen
each other for years – not since Simon's funeral. She used to
work with John and Adam in their London courier company,
but after they fell out she moved to Yorkshire where she set up
her own successful courier company with her boyfriend's

daughter, and now lives with him – an old medical colleague of our father – and their three-year-old son Matthew.

John and Jane are as relaxed together as they used to be, joking, kidding each other and playing tricks. It's as if the reason for their reconciliation doesn't exist. Their laughter puzzles the children; is their uncle ill or not?

We walk up the road to visit Oma. Our old grandmother says nothing about the AIDS, but jokes about how both she and John were in hospital at the same time with pneumonia. I think she does not say anything more specific because she does not understand.

It is hard to listen to them. Oma is now approaching her ninetieth birthday and will live for another two years. Her age and deteriorating eyesight have not stopped her tending her garden and buying new plants for her to admire 'in her old age'. John is not even thirty-five, and he is trying desperately to work out how to use the time he has left. In some ways he is physically more debilitated than Oma, and as a result of diarrhoea he has become very thin. He still frets about getting back to New York, but Adam has told him he must stay in London until his health is much better. Even flying before Christmas with pneumonia was dangerous, with the risk of a collapsed lung.

There is a hard frost. The branches of the trees and the plants in the garden are covered in a coat of white ice crystals. I am inside in the warm and through the French windows watch John walking around the garden, head down, his hands pushed deep into the pockets of his coat.

His hair is cut very short and the contours of his skull are so sharp that I want to draw them. His thinness makes the cheekbones jut out of his face like cliffs. He has chronic diarrhoea. For years John avoided tap water, but while in New York he thoughtlessly sipped some when drinking down medication. He assumes that this is how he got this infection of the intestine, which causes large amounts of fluid and nutrient loss. He talks about it as if it is some animal attached to him. 'My crypto is really bad at the moment,' he says, or 'My crypto is behaving itself recently.' There is no cure.

Watching John walking across the frosted lawn, I wonder what he is thinking, and wonder again what it's like to know that you will probably be dead within a few months. It is impossible to imagine your own death when you are healthy. But is it possible even if you know that you are terminally ill? I am healthy and fit; I cannot put myself into the mind of someone with full-blown AIDS and a death sentence. One day this year will be John's death day.

The year stretches ahead in my mind. How can we make plans? Again I think about our planned holidays – France in August, Thailand in November. Will they have to be cancelled at the last moment? There is nothing to be done. We have to live life as if it is normal, even though it sometimes feels selfish. Like the building work, we cannot put it on hold.

However, some things can be changed. Dick has been invited on a press trip to Israel for the *Guardian*, which involves his going away for ten days at the end of February. When he decides to cancel, I tell him he should not do this for my sake, but nevertheless I am relieved. I usually enjoy having a few days to myself when Dick goes away, but at the moment I feel a bit too feeble for it. And I can tell that Dick does not want to be away if John suddenly dies.

But in some respects things seem relatively stable, as John continues to meet me at my office once a week and we are able to lunch together.

One day, John arrives looking very excited because he has

received a friendly letter from Mark. While he was in the hospital he had specifically stated that he did not want to see Mark or Clare. Understandably offended by this, Mark didn't attempt to make contact with John at all. The relationship between these two brothers has been difficult for many years and it is hard for both of them to act as if nothing has ever happened.

But at last – now he knows about John's condition – Mark has taken the initiative and written. He is not the one waiting to die; in the circumstances, it is right that he should make the first move. Mark's three children have all been born since Simon's death and John has never seen them, so Mark suggests that he come round one evening soon.

John's joy at Mark's gesture is almost palpable. Always expecting people to reject him unless he showers gifts and attention on them, he is pathetically grateful.

A week later John comes to dinner with us at Falkland Road. After our children have gone to bed, we talk. He says he had a good evening with Mark and Clare and expresses his admiration for their new house. I ask what he thought of the children, his nieces and nephew. He looks blankly at me and says, 'Oh, they were already in bed when I got there.'

'What did they cook?' Mark is a good cook and enjoys rustling up interesting food.

John shrugs. 'Oh, they took me out to dinner.'

I can tell that he thinks there is nothing odd in what he has just told me, but to me it seems strange.

Why did they keep their children away from the uncle they have never met and take him out to dinner rather than have a more personal evening and a home-cooked meal? The first thought that crosses my mind is – were they afraid of contamination? My puzzlement grows. Even Oma and my Aunt

Barbara know that AIDS cannot be 'caught' from kissing or sharing cutlery.

On impulse I write to Mark and Clare, telling them in an oblique way that at this stage they should show John that he is loved regardless of his condition. I know my little brother. He has always felt there was no love left for him in such a large family, especially since he is not clever, and having HIV makes him feel even more unlovable.

I get a letter back from Mark and Clare telling me that I have spoiled what was to them a lovely evening with John. I think they've missed my point; I have certainly missed theirs.

On 1 February, I go to a huge party at the Imperial War Museum for the launch of Adam Sisman's biography of A.J.P. Taylor. Adam has had overwhelmingly good reviews for this, his first book, and I am proud of my friend. He always was a clever boy. I have known him since we were both seventeen years old, when he was at St Paul's Boys' School and I was at St Paul's Girls. Adam went out with my sister Jane for some time and, before he started writing, was a book publisher for many years.

Everyone is in a good mood. Lots of old friends are there – both personal and professional – and it is a relief to talk nothing but shop. I find myself in a corner talking to an old publishing friend who confides in me about her alcoholic sister and the problems her illness brings to the family. I don't want to talk about what bothers me, but I am always happy to listen to others' stories. It's a form of looking on the bright side – there's always someone in a worse situation than oneself.

On 8 February I go up to Liverpool to appear on 'This Morning', with Richard and Judy, to launch the *She*/Granada Short Story Competition which I have set up with producer James Hunt. Linda, who as editor would normally go, has another engagement, so as her deputy I have to take the train to Liverpool and stay overnight in order to appear on the programme the next morning.

The following weekend, Dick and I leave the children with Anne, the nanny – who moves into our house with her own children for two days – and set off for a rare weekend alone. We go to the West Country, visiting antiques shops and craft-men and -women, including Dorset potter Richard Batterham whom I have often visited with my grandmother. We buy lots of Batterham pots – lidded jars, functional bowls, a couple of studio pieces. They will make good presents, we tell ourselves, but we both know that we shall probably be unable to part with most of them, so perfect and pleasing are they.

Dick's parents, Norma and Eugene, arrive from New York to stay for a couple of weeks on their annual visit. They know my family well and are fond of John and Jacques, who come to dinner on my birthday, 14 February.

The following day I go to see *Der Rosenkavalier* at the Coliseum with my father. This is Peter's birthday present to me. Opera is an interest we share, as did Simon. Apart from dinner at Christmas and Easter, it is often only at the opera houses that we see each other during the year. We talk about John and I tell him about my rage at Mark and Clare. Peter always listens with interest, but stays out of any family disputes. It could be said that he has stayed out of his family life altogether.

The big birthday bash at Devonshire Place is held on 26 February half-way between my birthday and Adam's. It is a grand affair in the tall Adam drawing room where my mother used to see her patients, with the overspill into my father's former consulting room next door. People make jokes about how there is nothing to sit on except psychiatrists' couches. I laugh back. I have spent so many years living 'above the shop' that this had not occurred to me, but it is true. I had not even thought to put away the ECT equipment that lies on a table in the corner.

The guests are a good mix of writers, publishers, journalists and lawyers. Many are friends of both Adam and me, but there are plenty of others, including family. Adam's sister is over from New York. John and Jacques come. I have an odd sensation being in our old family house, where we all grew up and to which we are about to say goodbye, and seeing my little brother across the room to whom we shall also be saying goodbye before long.

I think of the story my mother tells about taking John and Adam to see this elegant house before we moved in. They (aged seven and nine), approved of it, they said, and the best things about it were the empty cupboards and the envelopes on the doormat with foreign stamps on them. Both excellent reasons for buying a house, of course!

John talks animatedly to my friends who know him. He has always been charming and good at talking to people on social occasions. There he is, a dying man, asking people questions, showing genuine interest in their lives, laughing and smiling. He is brave.

I stand in the doorway and look at the groups of people talk-ing, drinking, laughing and arguing. Some of them are getting very drunk. I have reached forty years of age and I feel guilty. Perhaps it is survivor guilt? I have made it, as Mark before me, but Simon died when he was thirty-eight; John is not going to reach forty – he may not even get to his thirty-fifth birthday in June.

And now the party is over. The build-up and the climax have passed. It is late February and the drama of the year still lies ahead of us.

I have been having a terrible time sleeping. I fall asleep, eager to block out the world, but then wake in the early hours worrying about John, my work and my book.

Long ago I decided that I must not use John's illness as an excuse for not doing the book I was commissioned to write. If I can write in these circumstances, I think, I can do so at any time. I write in longhand, with a Filofax, and I scribble it when I'm waiting for a train or to meet someone in a restaurant.

When I am not actually writing, I think about the current chapter I am working on and I jot down notes in spare moments. It helps to stop me thinking about John. But at night, it's impossible to block out the thoughts that churn around in my head. Deprived of sleep, I am often sluggish for most of the next day.

I visit my GP, Iona Heath, who listens to my story and asks me gently if I think I am depressed. I am shocked at the thought, but I know that it's not an outrageous suggestion; it just hadn't occurred to me. Dr Heath says she thinks I am – she could prescribe some anti-depressants that would not only improve my mood but also help me to sleep better. 'You've got a tough time ahead of you,' she says, 'and sometimes it is better to start getting prepared before the worst happens.'

In fact I am no stranger to depression. Four years ago in 1984, when I sank into a deep trough of gloom after my first miscarriage, it was Dr Heath who nudged me towards getting some psychological help. I was lucky to find myself in the hands of another medically qualified doctor who is gifted in the art of psychotherapy; Dr H. later saw me through another miscarriage.

I was thirty when I first saw this exceptional woman who does not use a word of jargon and employs the English language so carefully that her sentences can sound like poetry.

When Simon died, I went back to her for a little propping-up. Now I can see I may be headed there again, and I am only glad that I have already done so much groundwork with her. My experience with Dr H. has given me a profound respect for skilful psychotherapy. If I had not found her when I did, I think my life would have turned out very differently.

In spite of all this, I still find it hard to admit to needing help. I am ashamed, and my shame is a legacy of my upbringing. My parents' patients are the ones who are mentally ill, not their children – and especially not me, the competent big sister. But I know this is a delusion. Simon was severely ill with manic depression; I am aware that I am not as stable as I always thought. Fortunately I am rational enough to see the sense of it, but I know I shall not be able to tell anyone except Dick that I am taking anti-depressants. I am always regarded as a determined and tough fighter who gets what she wants; I am not seen as weak or vulnerable. Only Dick and a couple of very close friends know the truth. I sometimes wonder if it was the treatment by our sadistic nanny that enables me to function so well even when I am feeling bad inside. I just get on with things no matter what.

As it is, work is getting increasingly tough. In mid-March, as the April magazine hits the news-stands, we begin to receive a number of complaints about an article I wrote in the current issue to tie in with 'Take Your Daughters to Work Day'. In the article I suggested that girls should aim as high as possible in their education, to keep their options open. I gave as an example that it is better to aim to be a doctor than to settle for being a nurse. My comment has prompted numerous angry letters from nurses who tell me that nursing is a profession in its own right and that I have a nerve suggesting that it's not as good as medicine.

These complaints are addressed to Linda, as the editor. All letters from readers are answered, and she passes these on to me so that I can reply to them. Normally, I would think nothing about this and would simply write back to the readers with a simple justification of my article. Now I feel persecuted. At least two letters arrive every day for about ten days. Since we always reckon that for every reader who actually writes a letter there are ten more who mean to do so, I have visions of hundreds of angry nurses all over the country cursing me and hating me for my article. Thinking of John and those kind nurses who looked after him in the hospital, I am distressed at having upset them all, which was the last thing I wanted to do. I curse myself for not realising that this could happen. I could have given any other example if only I had thought about it.

Life is getting more and more difficult. I struggle to get through my days at the office, realising that I am hovering on the edge of disaster. I sit at my desk dreading the telephone ringing in case it brings yet another problem to add to the pile in my head, and I can feel myself tensing up every time someone approaches me with a question. Work crowds in on me, but I have to keep going. I must appear in control, mature and professional. Six o'clock comes round each evening as a welcome relief when I can leave the office and allow my thoughts to focus on what is really going on in my head.

The anti-depressants started to work after a couple of weeks and I have certainly been sleeping better. But I find it almost impossible to concentrate in meetings and have to write down everything that's said, otherwise I forget immediately. At times I feel as though I'm wading through deep mud, all my movements slowed down.

In addition to all this, the magazine is also in difficulty. The circulation figures are static, even falling; Linda is under increasing pressure from the managing director to boost circulation. The features editor leaves and we must look for somebody to fill that position. I am aware that I am not initiating things as I should; I am doing my job, but no more. I feel bad about it, but there is nothing I can do for the time being.

By the third week in March, I feel that everything is collapsing in on me. The stupid pills have not had a miraculous effect at all, but they do help me to just about function at work, and I struggle to keep on top of things there.

As part of the drive to increase *She's* circulation, focus groups have been set up to find out why people aren't buying the magazine. I have been diligent about going to all of these groups, spending long evenings sitting in a stuffy room in Primrose Hill and observing (through a two-way mirror) women talking about the magazine and what they do or don't like about it. Apart from finding this boring, I am cynical about the value of the entire exercise, which is costing my company plenty of money. It seems to me that only a very peculiar person would voluntarily spend an entire evening sitting in a windowless room with a group of strangers giving her opinion about the contents of a magazine. My brother is dying and I am spending my evenings like this?

Anxiety begins to become a daily experience. I have never had panic attacks before, but now I get flashes as I stand on the tube platform and at times have a terrifying urge to jump in front of the train as it roars into the station.

Not knowing what to do, I return to Dr Heath who suggests I take a week off. I feel feeble about it, but also too fragile to complain. She is right. I need some time to get in control, or else I shall have a serious crash.

When I tell Linda that I have to be signed off for a week, I can tell she is not delighted. I feel guilty about leaving her at this point when we should be putting everything into the magazine to turn it round. But I have no choice.

At home, I spend a few days pottering around doing practical chores. I cannot write. I speak to John on the telephone several times.

'You're spending a lot of time at home,' he comments one day.

I say nothing. I don't want to admit that I am so upset about his condition that I have to take time off work. My role as his big sister prevents me from telling him the truth. In fact, I don't tell anyone in the family that I am on sick leave. I pretend that I am just working at home.

When my week is up, I return to the office feeling much stronger and better, ready to face both work and John's future. I put on a cheerful face and make the decision not to talk about my personal life at all. However, on that first day Linda comes over to my desk. Looking anxious, she asks me to go out to have a cup of tea with her.

We sit in Cranks restaurant across the road.

'I need to know what's going on,' she says. Then she waits.

I can hardly believe my ears. 'What's going on?' I repeat her question. 'I thought you knew. My brother is dying,' I say, 'and he's still dying.'

In spite of my incredulity, I know that Linda is under great pressure herself. She tells me that I have to comment more on the direction of the magazine.

'I need you,' she says, 'and you're not here for me.'

Feeling threatened, I point out that I was the only member of staff to attend all the focus groups that were held late into the night several weeks earlier.

Finally, she gets round to it: 'What about this novel?'

'The novel is the only thing that keeps me going,' I say quietly.

This is true. By now the novel has become my true escape from the world. I cannot stop John dying but I can make my characters do as I say. For the past few weeks my book has been the only place where I have had any control at all.

By the time we return to the office I am fuming and astonished by what I take to be my friend's lack of understanding. I realise why it has happened, but this does not make it any easier for me.

I spend the afternoon writing a savage critique of the magazine – pouring my rage into it, ripping apart the articles and the design. It's just a superficial women's magazine anyway, I think. John's dying and I earn my living by feeding women's fantasies. I print it out and read it, then I tone it down before shoving it at Linda.

Linda looks pleased. She believes that her tactic has worked and that my mind is back on the job.

From then on I feel very alone at work, isolated from my colleagues. Making a painfully conscious effort to act as though I do not have a care in the world, I smile and speak in a pseudo-bright voice; I make jokes in editorial meetings, which come out as horribly cynical. Yet all the time I feel angry and desperate to run away from it all. I am also afraid now of losing my job. Linda's questioning has made me feel paranoid, so I feel that I can't afford to take any more time off without making my position vulnerable. I must sit it out.

While all this is going on, I still have lunch with John every week when he travels into the West End and meets me at my office. He is getting even thinner, and this is accentuated by his short haircut. His skin has a grey tinge to it. He looks ill and it seems to me obvious that he has AIDS. I am slightly self-conscious as we eat in the pizzeria in Beak Street and wonder if anyone else thinks the same. He always orders the same dish of mozzarella and tomatoes, but he rarely eats more than half of it. I think of us children when we were small, all wolfing down our food. Johnny was once sent home from his nursery school because he had not asked for seconds at lunch. His teacher, Miss Herbertson – who, my mother always said, understood exactly what went on in the minds of little boys – knew that he must be sickening for something. Indeed, he came down with chicken-pox the next day.

One week John sits down in the restaurant and tells me that he is glad to be HIV-positive. 'It gives me a perspective of the world that I wouldn't have otherwise.'

I smile and say nothing. Of course, he is right about having a different perspective on the world, but it strikes me as a desperately sad attempt to be brave.

Another day we talk about suicide. 'I'm not going through to the bitter end,' he says. 'I'm too vain. I don't want to end up looking like those people in Charles Bell. My looks are about the only thing I have.'

John has always thought he is stupid, but I don't feel that this is the time to boost him by telling him he has a wonderfully original intelligence, uncontaminated by the school system. I want to discuss suicide with him. I wait for him to tell me what he is planning, assuming that he has got the right information about how to kill himself through the gay network. I imagine he is about to tell me how he has got it all worked out.

As we talk, however, I realise that he has not got a clue. He knows he should do it when his quality of life has deteriorated. He has thought about how important it is to get the timing right, to act before he is too ill to carry it off, before he is left in the hands of the doctors and nurses who will simply prolong his existence until the very end. What he has not thought about is the means.

It is clear that John is asking for my advice. I am his big sister, he expects me to come to the rescue, so I try. I tell him that he has to build up a stash of sleeping pills. I talk about the Exit method of taking them with whisky and placing a bag over your head, but I don't think he is listening. Bruno Bettelheim killed himself this way, and it is what I would do if it came to it. I have always had an element of gloom inside me, usually kept well hidden from the world. It is not a secret, but it is private. I am sure that the reasons for this are complex – and there is plenty of depressive illness in the family genes – but I also have no doubt that the childhood experience with the nanny made a massive contribution too. I suspect that John also harbours plenty of depressive feelings beneath that cheerful exterior, for the same reasons.

Clearly John does not think that the moment for killing himself is imminent, because he now tells me that he is anxious to get back to New York. It is understandable. He does not belong to London any more: although he does not enjoy New York very much and has found it hard to make friends, his work and home are there. He insists that he is fit enough to travel.

When I speak to Adam on the telephone that night, I can tell that he is not happy about John returning to New York. He does not feel he is well enough. Nonetheless, he has found a large apartment to rent that belongs to the singer Bonnie Raitt. If John is going to come back, they should take a place together for the time being so that Adam can keep an eye on him.

John prepares to fly back to New York. As we say goodbye, I wonder if I'll ever see him again. He could get too ill to travel home and he might die there. I wonder briefly about what would happen. Would we bring his body back home or all fly out to New York for a funeral there?

Fourteen years earlier, in 1980, Dick and I were living in New York and we got married there at his parents' house in Mamaroneck, a leafy suburb of New York City. It was in the days of Freddie Laker's Sky Train, and cheap flights. Most of my family (apart from my father, for whom airline travel is difficult, and Adam who was spending a year in Australia) and several friends had all flown out for the occasion then; it had seemed wonderfully decadent to fly over for a wedding. A funeral would be different, though.

The weekend after John's departure, I go to stay with my grandmother for the weekend. My Aunt Barbara, who lives next door and is Oma's 'carer', is keen to go away. For the past seven years, Oma and I have gone away together for two-night breaks a couple of times a year. It was a chance for her to have a holiday and for Barbara to have a break, also an opportunity for me to have some time with Oma by myself.

I spent much of my childhood staying with Oma; she is an essential part of my life. Our travels together began when she first took me abroad to Venice and Florence. I was fifteen, and she thought I ought to spend less time with my horses and see some of the world.

At first our trips away were very active. We went to stay in a cottage on the Sissinghurst estate, or a hotel next to Tintern Abbey; we went round churches in Gloucestershire and bird-watching in Norfolk. We visited my cousin down in Exeter University and old friends of Oma's in Budleigh Salterton, Devon. We travelled the country looking at Roman villas and visiting bird sanctuaries. Most of all she liked to visit craftsmen and craftswomen – potters (such as Richard Batterham), weavers, basket makers – people she knew from her own involvement in the craft world.

They were fun, these trips. Oma was always good company,

but I would also relish the times when she took a nap in the afternoon and I was free to wander round second-hand bookshops or antiques shops in the towns we visited, or simply to lie on my hotel bed and read.

Now, sadly, Oma is less mobile and is not happy to stay away from home, so the solution is for me to go and stay with her and take her out on day trips from the house. That weekend I take her to Pallant House in Chichester. Although there is an entrance with a lift for the disabled, Oma insists on climbing the steep stone steps to the front door. We admire the paintings on the walls and visit the old kitchen. Then we look at the exhibition of rag rugs. Oma manages it all. She is extraordinary; I feel proud to have her blood in my veins.

But at supper that evening Oma lets it be known that she is cross about the original secrecy over John's condition. I try to explain that it was John's secret, that we had no alternative but to keep quiet. But she does not accept that; she believes that it affects the whole family and so everyone should know. I realise she thinks that, as the matriarch, she has a right to know everything that goes on.

There can be no agreement. But I can tell that she is confused about what AIDS is (she refers to it as AIMS), and what it means for John to have it. She has no idea what lies in store for him as he approaches death. None of us knows exactly, but she hasn't got a clue.

There is no explaining, so I change the subject as soon as I can and feel upset at the friction the discussion has caused.

In the middle of the night I listen to Oma getting up to go to the lavatory, and I can hear her listening to the World Service on the radio by her bed. Does she go to bed each night wondering if she will wake up the next morning? A few years ago I asked her about this. 'No,' she replied, as if it had never occurred to her. More likely, she didn't want to talk about it.

I wonder how much Oma thinks about death and how different her thoughts are from John's. What a difference, to have reached this point after a long and fruitful life rather than when you're in your early thirties. I fall asleep wondering how John is getting on in New York and what it will be like if I wake up and find Oma dead in her bed the next morning.

That Sunday night, I am back in London with Dick and the children when Adam calls from New York to say that he is not happy about John's condition. Apparently John arrived in New York looking even more ill than Adam had expected: 'He was wearing a grey top and his face was almost the same colour. He's also got very thin.' It is painful to hear Adam saying that John has some demented idea about having lots of sex while he still can. I recall John's comment about being 'glad' to be HIV-positive, and wonder if it is just an excuse for all his hedonism and his desire for instant gratification without responsibility. 'It's pathetic,' Adam says. 'All his looks are eroded and he is decidedly unsexy with it.'

A few days after that, Adam brings John home. New York was evidently a disaster for them both.

The New York business is frantically busy. Adam has spent so much time coming backwards and forwards to London that it is getting out of control, and he has been running it single-handed anyway. In addition, a lot of time and energy are being taken up with a lawsuit going on against a former employee who launched his own business out of A-Z. Adam has been struggling to keep everything on course but at the same time pretending that he is not too busy to spend time with John, to make him feel better. John has heard about a miracle drug for the crypto and wants to wait to get his hands on it. It then turns out that he is already taking the drug, though under another name.

Adam tells us that he argued with John about coming home. John did not want to return at all, but Adam almost dragged him on to the plane to England. John was throwing up every few minutes on the flight, but fortunately one of the air stewards was someone whom Adam (a frequent flier) knew. The steward quickly realised what was going on and ushered them both into a quiet spot in business class where John's vomiting and unsteadiness would be less likely to disturb anyone.

So now John is home again in London. He will not return to the United States. It seems like the first 'never again' before he dies. Adam is reeling from the expense of getting the flights home and worried about the amount of time he has spent away from the business. He is even more worried about the legal fees mounting up for the impending court case. His lawyers are not working on a contingency basis, either.

Exhausted by John's last stay in town, I am rather unprepared to have him back so soon. I had hoped to have a breathing space. This one will be the last, and we do not know how long it will be. Whatever the case, we have to find a way of keeping John happy here in London.

Chapter Five

April

Back at the house in Kentish Town, the work has begun and the builders are going great guns. It is oddly exciting to see such destruction. They have ripped down the whole of the back extension, the old Victorian scullery, and now there is dust everywhere. The boiler stays in place but wrapped up in plastic to protect it from the elements; the lavatory bowl stares up at the open sky. It is wonderful to think that these bricks, now carefully stacked up against the wall ready to be used again, were first laid by labourers over one hundred years ago, when the world was a very different place.

For the first few weeks I am delighted by these builders of ours. They are reliable, professional, hard-working and careful to clear up after themselves each day. They are also cheerful and kind to the children; Ruth particularly likes the youngest one, Paul, and sits on the front step each day waiting for him. I recommend them to my friends. One weekend, the boiler packs up during a night storm and Dave comes over that Sunday morning to get it going again. He looks a bit rough after a late Saturday night but, after he has fixed it and we thank him for his trouble, he says firmly, 'While this work is going on, I am responsible for anything that is affected by it.'

I feel in good hands, and safe.

But, of course, it can't last. About a week later, Dave mentions in passing that he is going off on holiday in the Caribbean for two weeks. 'I need the break,' he says casually.

When I look surprised, he quickly says, 'Oh, I thought I'd told you. I know I told Phil. Besides, I owe it to myself,' he adds defensively. He tells me too that he is taking his eight-year-old boy – during term, I note disapprovingly.

There's nothing to be done. I can see that the original estimated six weeks of work are likely to stretch well into the summer.

A fortnight later Dave returns, relaxed after his holiday. Now his behaviour changes and I suspect he has another job elsewhere. For although one of his team turns up most days, Dave's own presence is rare. My enthusiasm for our builders fades rapidly, but fortunately I feel so anxious about John that these troubles about the extension seem trivial.

The big question now is – what is John going to do with himself? What do you do when you are waiting to die? I had never thought about it. As a child, you think that people are either alive or dead. Simon was alive one minute and a moment later unquestionably dead. I have never wondered about people walking around while they are dying, while their bodies are packing up on them. Of course, that is what we all do throughout life. It's just speeded up for the terminally ill, for whom the clock is closer to winding down.

But John needs to fill his days in some way. He may feel like lying hopelessly in bed but he could still be going strong for weeks, or even months. It is difficult to imagine what he feels. In his position, I think I would constantly be saying, 'What's the point?'

Dick suggests that John try psychotherapy. We agree that it might keep him occupied, as well as helping him control the feelings he probably can't talk about to his friends. John seems interested and a doctor friend gives us the name of someone who can help. It takes a while but finally, through a gay organisation, we get the name of a therapist in East Finchley for John to visit. At first he is keen on it and goes once or twice a week. I am surprised to hear that the therapist expects to be paid in cash after every session. I suppose with terminally ill clients you don't know if you will see them again, but it still strikes me as a little rough.

After a few weeks, frequent trips into the hospital and consequent exhaustion mean that John has to miss sessions, and he is losing interest. Nothing is said, but I sense that the psychotherapy has not lived up to its early promise. My brother is neither very verbal nor particularly introspective, so the 'talking cure' does not hold his attention for long. Also, he has always tended to lose interest in things quickly, so this is nothing new. However, he still goes for occasional sessions and maintains contact with the therapist.

Back home in Alwyne Road, John has bought himself a Russian Blue kitten he names Tsar. This is typical extravagance. Nowadays, when he wants something it has to be the best and the most expensive. The cat must have cost at least two hundred pounds, which he and Jacques can hardly afford. But I must admit it is very cute, and will be company for him. The children are delighted when we go round one Saturday afternoon to play with this bouncy dusty-blue ball of fur.

John has always liked cats. At Devonshire Place we had a massive black cat named Archibald which just walked into the house one day and stayed. A magnificent creature, resembling a miniature puma, he liked to sleep curled up on the sofa in the waiting room, causing some of the more nervous patients to ask the secretaries if he was dangerous.

When Archibald died, John and Adam went in search of a replacement cat and came back with Humphrey, a black-and-white kitten, hand-picked by the boys from a litter in Camden Town. Humphrey had a scruffiness about him which showed that his mother had not taught him to wash himself, and he walked with a scissors gait that our mother said was the sign that he had cerebral palsy.

At first Humphrey was a great success, following the boys everywhere like a dog. Then one day they took him to a park and suddenly, without warning, Humphrey sank his teeth into Adam's arm. From then on, he was prone to unprovoked outbursts of hissing and spitting that sent him flying round the room like a rogue firework. To most people, he was unattractive and unlovable; even Dick, a great cat lover, could not see the point of him. But John loved him, looked after him and kept him long after he moved away from Devonshire Place and had his own home.

One day John talks about the house and the mortgage. He says that he and Jacques have not been able to keep up the payments and the bank has been threatening to repossess the property. They have renegotiated the instalments several times and now, because of John's health, the bankers have agreed on compassionate grounds to wait before initiating repossession orders.

Since the bottom has fallen out of the property market and the house is worth far less than the mortgage, the bank may simply have decided to delay until the market picks up before acting. Whatever the case, this is a relief. It means that while John is alive, he has a place to live – even if Jacques will have to find another home for himself on John's death.

Easter is difficult, as it has been ever since 1989 when Simon died. As always, Dick and I are down in Sussex for the holiday. Sunday is the day when the children have their Easter-egg hunt in the garden while the grown-ups enjoy their drinks before an Easter lunch. It is also the anniversary of Simon's death, the day he shot himself five years ago. In my head Simon has two death dates – 26 March and Easter Sunday. Every Easter Sunday at 6 o'clock I think about coming in through the gates of Wiblings and seeing Simon lying on the lawn. Now these thoughts are muddled by John's condition.

The following weekend, it is my grandmother's ninetieth birthday and a large lunch party has been planned at her house. Jane is away in France with Matthew; Mark and his family are in the Canary Islands for the holiday. John and I are the only Dally grandchildren present, my children the only great-grand-children. There is to be a speech by one of my mother's oldest friends, John Hughes. A retired GP, John has known Oma since he was four and is famous in our family for having thrown a worm into our mother's mouth as a child. What a good shot, we always thought!

As the eldest granddaughter, I make a toast. The sun shines and we all spill out into the garden. There are lots of cousins, close and distant, from four generations, and many friends as well as people from the village. Oma sits in a chair on the ter-race talking to her visitors while John, looking extremely gaunt, is hunched in a chair near her. My father, Oma's ex-son-in-law, sits down between them; Peter is uneasy in social situations and seems hunched with shyness. Three generations hunched in a row . . .

But the party is a success. Oma seems pleased to be the centre of attention and it is wonderful to see the little children running round and so many senior cousins paying tribute to her, the family matriarch. So she should be pleased. Here is a woman who used to stand on her head every morning until her eighties; who taught herself to weave and became a bene-factor to the crafts. She and my Aunt Barbara used to run a crafts centre here in Graffham, teaching fabric weaving, spin-ning, pottery and basket-weaving to local adults and children. With some of her inherited wealth Oma set up a trust in her name, the Gwen Mullins Trust, which allocated money to craftsmen and craftswomen in need before the Craft Council even existed.

As I stand on the lawn on that sunny party day surrounded by our vast extended family, I think of my great-grandmother, Oma's mother, who came to Europe from Savannah, Georgia, at the end of the nineteenth century to escape a society scandal. Travelling in Egypt, chaperoned by her mother, she had met Augustus Brandt, a Russian-German who lived in England and ran a merchant bank with his brothers.

The family story says that Augustus's conservative German family in Heidelburg were concerned to hear about this not-so-young American woman their eldest son wanted to marry. They sent one of his brothers over to check her. A famous telegram came back from him: 'IF GUSSIE DOESN'T MARRY HER, I WILL.'

When Dick and I lived in New York, I spent many hours in the New York Public Library, and discovered the truth about the events that brought our ancestor across the Atlantic to a new life abroad. It was quite trivial but a good society scandal plastered all over the *New York Times* in the 1890s, and I decided to write a novel about it one day.

Now here we all are, all the different branches of the family. Lennox Money, Oma's nephew, places a portrait of Oma's father, Augustus Brandt, on a chair in the sitting room. It is a copy of one painted by Philip de Laszlo in the 1920s, and he has brought it down for his sister Diana, who is also present. His other sister, Elizabeth, committed suicide in the sixties. I remember when it happened; I was staying with Oma and there was a lot of talk among the adults about Elizabeth having died. I was not told the truth at the time, but I guessed, and I worried about the two little children she had left behind.

I used to pore over my grandmother's family photo albums and imagine myself in that world of wealth and privilege. Now when I look at photographs of Elizabeth as a little girl, playing at their grandparents' house in Bletchingly with my mother and Barbara, her cousins, I can see only unhappiness in her face. She is never smiling. Perhaps there will be another family story to write about one day.

Suicide. Sitting next to his father Peter in the sunshine, John is not smiling. At some point soon he means to kill himself. You cannot gas yourself as in the old days, like our cousin Elizabeth and Sylvia Plath. No oven for John. No gun, either. The police took away Simon's shotgun – and anyway it would not be in John's nature to shoot himself. He is too gentle. A friend whose father shot himself through the heart said that he was proud of his looks and would never have damaged them by shooting himself in the head. But perhaps he was too far gone for vanity; someone said that suicides destroy the part that hurts them most. Did Simon's brain hurt?

For all its strangeness, I like being with this family of mine – all these different people who have a genetic connection. It gives you a reason to talk and communicate. Sometimes it works, sometimes it doesn't, but there is something special about it. I drink some more champagne and begin to feel guilty about my anger at Mark and Clare. I have a tendency to expect people to conform to excessively high standards – set by myself, naturally. I know I should be a little more flexible and a lot less critical.

So I find myself thinking of ways to smooth the path, to communicate with Mark and Clare so as to end the enmity between us. I can no longer bear to be at odds with them. I realise to my relief that I have the perfect 'peg' – as we call it in the magazine world – in Clare's approaching birthday.

I write to Clare wishing her a happy birthday. After a while, she writes back. The path is cleared for civil communication again.

Meanwhile, I am keen for my children to see as much of John as possible; they are fond of their uncle, who has always been fun and generous to them. They are clearly confused about the situation and find it odd that he has not died yet. 'When is he going to die?' Rebecca asks.

Alice is also perplexed. 'If he's going to die, why does he have that nice smile on his face all the time?'

'Because he enjoys seeing you,' I reply.

John and Jacques come to supper one night. John has been out of hospital for a while and he manages to drink champagne and eat. But suddenly in the middle of the meal, he starts to sob; the sobbing turns violent, and his lips are pulled back over his teeth as he tries to control it. My instinct is to get up and hug him but I hang back and let Jacques do it.

Jacques stands behind him to rub his chest. 'Are you in pain?'

John nods. 'It's my chest,' he says. 'The medication makes it hurt.'

Dick calls a minicab to take John and Jacques home. The abrupt end to what had been a pleasant evening is unsettling. I do not think my brother is crying in pain; I think he is weeping tears of fear, and there is nothing that any of us can do to make him feel better.

John is admitted to hospital again for a brief spell. The doctors are not sure if he has pneumonia or not. Why can't they tell?

I visit him again after work. Opposite him is a man surrounded by a group of cheerful-sounding friends. The patient himself looks quite healthy. 'He's going home tomorrow,' says John. 'He works at the opera house.'

An elderly man sits in the next bed, his wife at his side. They look as if they come from the Home Counties. He reads the *Daily Telegraph* and looks remarkably sanguine about his fate. His wife looks calm, too. I am impressed. This man is proof that AIDS affects everyone, I think. It is not just a gay disease, as people like to believe. Of course, I know that he could be gay, but the calm presence of his respectable-looking wife suggests otherwise.

'When did he come in?' I whisper to John. My curiosity is firing on all cylinders.

John shrugs. 'He arrived yesterday. I don't know anything about him yet.'

Two days later when I visit, the man has gone. I ask John about him, eager to find out how he contracted HIV.

'Oh, that was a mistake,' he says. 'For some reason he was brought into the wrong ward.'

John tells me that Princess Diana came to visit them all late one night. He was impressed. I am fairly impressed too. After all, this confirms what has been rumoured in the press anyway. Diana actually did make these nocturnal visits; they were not just concocted by her press office, as some people believe. But one thing the Princess of Wales has done annoys me. When she was recently filmed visiting an AIDS ward with her sons, TV cameras in tow, it was reported that instead of telling the boys the truth about these patients, she told them that they were dying of cancer. I feel this is unnecessarily dishonest. I don't say anything to John, though. He likes Princess Diana and, after all, Jacques makes some of her dresses.

When I ask John if many people in the ward have died, he looks at me as though it is a stupid question. 'Oh, loads of them,' he says flippantly. 'The nurses always ask if we'd like the curtains drawn around our beds while they wheel out the corpses on a trolley.' He shrugs his broad but bony shoulders. 'I shan't be here when it's my turn,' he adds.

Early in May, John is out of hospital again and keen to get away with Jacques for a week or so. He asks me for a brochure I have for self-catering country cottages. During the same conversation, he talks about suicide again. He has the pills now, he says; he got plenty in America, and he has been thinking about it. But he is not planning to tell anyone when he is about to do it. He won't be saying goodbye, it will be too difficult.

I imagine that he is planning to rent a cottage and commit suicide in some remote part of England. Again I start worrying about the practicalities of such an event. I lend him the brochure, but nothing comes of it.

In the middle of May, I go to the fortieth birthday party of my friend Judy Williamson in Highgate. Judy, an academic and writer, is an old friend from St Paul's. At school she was always known as the cleverest girl in our year and got away with a great deal of naughtiness because of it, but was finally expelled for scratching 'Fuck the Public School System' on a door at the brand-new boys' school across the river. Nevertheless, she went on to achieve brilliant 'A' Levels from a sixth-form college, and then a First at Sussex University.

Jude comes from a family of six children, too, so we have always had a great deal in common.

I spot an old boyfriend I have not seen in years, and we catch up on the news about each other's families. His mother is still alive but his father died a few years ago, and he tells me about his brother with whom I used to go on anti-apartheid demonstrations many years ago. In turn I tell him about John, whom he remembers as a pesky twelve-year-old little brother. My ex-boyfriend also confides that his father, whom I remember well, sexually abused him as a child. I listen with great interest but a feeling of deep gloom. I remember his father as a creep. I leave early and am pleased to climb into bed.

Back at work the book publishing party season is in full swing. I have not been accepting many invitations recently, but I cannot resist the party for Maya Angelou at the Reform Club. Years ago, in 1985 – when I was on *Cosmopolitan* and before Maya was famous in this country – I published an extract from *I Know Why the Caged Bird Sings* in the magazine, and invited her to talk at the *Cosmo* Book Day which I organised each autumn. Maya was magnificent. She electrified the lecture hall at City University, talking in that deep gravelly voice with its mesmerising Southern drawl. Although the rest of the line-up of authors was impressive, no one matched the effect of Maya Angelou.

Marina Warner was scheduled to speak after her. 'My God, it's like going on after the Beatles!' she wailed.

Maya Angelou is fêted wherever she goes now. Here at the Reform Club the party is grand. I am pleased to see several old friends from the book world, but much of the time I feel very detached. Someone quizzes me about my father, alerting me immediately to the fact that she was a patient at Devonshire Place. I can often tell who is a patient. Once a well known magazine editor told me that it was her ambition to be a patient of Peter's.

The house in Devonshire Place has been sold now and the furniture is being erratically distributed amongst the children. There is a table my mother had in her nursery as a child, which the housekeeper painted white years ago, and my mother wants it stripped and polished. Dick mentions this to Dave, the builder, who says he has a mate who will renovate the table for fifty pounds. It is brought up to our house and Dave takes it away with him for his friend to fix up for us. So easy. We're grateful to him.

But I wish Dave would get a move on with the building work. Some days the builders are there; some days not. Sometimes I get angry and worked up about it; sometimes, I let it wash over me. It is not easy to see much difference on a daily basis, but I reckon they work a couple of hours every day and no more.

The half-term is coming up and the writer Victoria Glendinning is lending us her house in southern Ireland for the week. Her husband, Terence, has had Parkinson's disease for some years and now has dementia. On 24 May when I go round in the evening to pick up the key to her house, Terence is upstairs in bed; they have just come back from Ireland, but it was clearly a difficult trip with him in that condition. Victoria looks tired and sad.

When I was literary editor of *Cosmopolitan*, I asked her to be the magazine's book reviewer, which she continued for several years. She has also spoken about writing biographies at one of my *Cosmo* Book Days. I tell her about John. Terence is dying. John is dying. Victoria has four sons, somewhat younger than John but, like him, tall, handsome young men. Unlike him, young men with their whole lives ahead of them.

Before we go I telephone John to say goodbye. He says that he and Jacques are heading off for a hotel in Greece for ten days. I am pleased that he feels well enough to go and, in an odd way, glad that he will be out of the country at the same time as we are.

We go to Ireland on the boat. It is a good week. Victoria's house is a beautiful old converted chapel surrounded by lush green fields. There is a small wood with paths which run down to the river where trout flash their silver bellies in the sunlight and leap provocatively out of the water. Cows graze in the fields beyond and the wild garlic scents the air.

We meet groups of English friends who have come here for every holiday of their lives. Dick is not in a sociable mood, and I can see it is easy to get locked into a timetable of social rounds which defeats the purpose of a holiday. Besides, he is anxious about a pilot programme for a radio food quiz show that he has been involved in. He speaks to the producer several times on the telephone. It looks as though we shall have to leave a day early for him to get to the recording.

Our days are relaxing. Sometimes we drive down to the coast to walk by the seashore and throw stones into the water. The children love it. We eat wonderful food and drink delicious beer. Back at the house I paint pictures with the girls. We read and play table tennis in the large echoing room that used to be the chapel.

The evenings seem to go on until midnight, as the light fades so slowly in the West. I work on my book and play baseball with the children. The house is warm and welcoming, with a kitchen range and a small sitting room filled with books. The conservatory, where we spend most of our time when indoors, is bright and light. The floor is painted a Mediterranean blue and exotic cacti and other succulents flourish in deep beds.

Victoria is a keen and gifted gardener. I water her plants diligently, as requested. But there is a sadness about the house, too. Aware that Victoria and Terence have just had their last visit there together, the sight of Terence's Wellington boots under the bench and his large straw hat hanging on the hook by the back door makes my chest tighten with sorrow.

One evening we eat freshly caught lobster for supper, and one day make a trip out to Baltimore where we catch the ferry over to Sherkin Island. As we sit in the boat, the children exclaim at the seals slumped on the rocks that we pass. Arriving at Sherkin, I think about John and my sister Jane who came camping here as teenagers some twenty years ago. I imagine them walking along the tiny narrow road with the masses of wild orchids in the grass verges. The image is almost overwhelming. Am I to be reminded of John wherever I go, whatever I do?

We return to England on the ferry from Cork to Swansea. The boat is scheduled to arrive at 8.00 in the evening; instead it docks at 1 o'clock in the morning, as a raging storm prevents it from entering the harbour for hours. It is terrifying. The passengers squeal with fear and excitement as another lurch of the ship sends the crockery sliding off the tables – just like the movies, I think. Even the staff look alarmed. It is difficult to walk around the keeling boat, so we sit on the floor with our backs to the wall. Only Ruth, whose centre of gravity is so low, can walk around without losing balance.

We were planning to drive straight home to London, but by the time the boat eventually docks it is far too late. Exhaustion forces us to book into a hotel in Swansea, making it a rather expensive ending to our holiday. We vow never to risk the Irish Sea again.

The next morning, Dick goes off to Birmingham to record

the pilot quiz show and I drive the children home to London. In spite of the storm, the air remains close.

Back home, I am disappointed and annoyed to find that the building work has *still* not progressed very much, if at all. How foolish of me to imagine that Dave would use our week away to get a lot of things done! The laziness of the builders depresses me, but I fight the feeling. I have just had a good holiday and need to save my energy for the weeks ahead. So I avert my eyes from the mess and ignore it.

John is still away, so I don't have to fret about him but can imagine him sitting in the sun on a beach somewhere in Greece. The coming Monday is 6 June, VE Day and his thirty-fifth birthday, so he has made it half-way to threescore and ten. How are he and Jacques planning to celebrate?

Dick returns from Birmingham, confident that the recording went well. He was the quiz master, with the panellists Clarissa Dickson-Wright, Nigel Slater and Sophie Grigson. Now they have to see if the BBC producers like what they have done.

On Sunday morning I wheel Ruth down the road in the buggy to return the key to Victoria, taking a bottle of champagne as a thank-you present. As I open the gate, I can see her sitting in the garden with someone else. She jumps to her feet and comes over; I sense that she does not want me to come in. It is clearly not a good time. Terence is dying. 'It's close to the end,' she says.

I do not know what to say. The champagne seems a totally inappropriate present in the circumstances, but I thrust it into her hands anyway. Thanking her profusely, I back the buggy out of the garden and return home, shocked by the encounter. I was so unprepared. I find myself wondering what Victoria meant when she said it was 'close to the end'. What did this mean exactly? *How* does one know? Will it be the same for John as for Terence?

If I had lived a hundred years ago I would not be wondering like this. Seeing dead people is a rare occurrence for people outside hospitals nowadays. I have already seen one dead person in my life. I suppose I shall see John's dead body, too.

A few days later I read Terence's obituaries in the paper and I send Victoria a note. It is not the same for her, I know. I am simply a sibling; Victoria has lost her husband.

John is back from Greece and comes to supper, without Jacques. He has a wonderful sun-tan but he is also very thin; the crypto is bad. He says he did not do much in Greece, he did not feel well enough to go out of the hotel room. Jacques was very kind and devotedly stayed to look after him much of the time rather than go out to enjoy himself. John says that he forgot about his birthday and did not remember it until the next day. This strikes me as unbearably sad, but he has other things on his mind. He is worried about his sight; he says that for some time he has had blurry vision in his left eye.

A visit to the hospital the next day confirms that John now has cytomegalovirus (CMV) of the eye – a serious infection that will progress and cause loss of vision, sometimes in both eyes. This is familiar to me. Derek Jarman went blind with this same virus, when he made his movie *Blue*. Treatment is by drugs given intravenously. John says they will put in a Hickman line, so that he can be given the medication more easily. This seems terrifying. He will have this tube in his chest for ever – whatever 'for ever' is now. In my mind it is beginning to be coupled with 'never again'.

But John's CMV gives us some sense of timing. He has been told that the drugs can ward off the blindness for nine months, no more. I remember that when he was about nine, he had a blind friend at school. Wanting to know what life was like for his friend, he once spent several hours over a weekend with a furry Davy Crockett hat pulled down over his eyes, feeling his way around Devonshire Place in order to experience life without sight.

We talk about suicide again. Well, he is certainly not going to allow himself to go blind. Nine months. No more than nine months?

Some days John and Jacques still manage supper at our house. Sometimes they beg off when John is not feeling well. He is an invalid now. At times I think we are his only social life, but I know that's not true because he has plenty of good friends. Perhaps we are the only ones able and happy to provide a regular home-cooked meal. Dick does all the cooking in our house, and he likes to produce a decent meal every night. Now John is registered as disabled, he qualifies for extra help from the Council: he can claim for taxi rides to the hospital, and home helps are sent round to help with the housework. Jacques and John talk about these people who come to the house three times a week; one of them gives them the creeps, they say, but they are too embarrassed to complain to the Council about him.

On Sunday, 12 June, the telephone rings at 5.30 a.m. I jerk myself awake and grab the receiver, convinced that a call at this hour can only bring bad news. It is John; he is ringing to say that he has realised just how much we all love him. He sounds both upset and high.

I put down the phone but I cannot get back to sleep. We are not a sentimental family and I am convinced that this was a coded message, a final goodbye from my brother. I spend an anxious day waiting to telephone; I don't want to sound too worried. When I ring, Jacques says John is having a nap but is fine. Just a false alarm.

Day to day, life is getting harder for John. Chronically tired, constantly having to take naps, his weeks are filled with visits to the hospital. His crypto is now out of control; he confesses with shame that he even leaks at night, which must be so humiliating.

On 16 June, it is a beautiful balmy evening. When John comes to supper – this time without Jacques, who probably wants an evening to himself – he is in a cheerful mood. He laughs at our static building work and the mess in the garden that prevents us from sitting out there. Then he goes upstairs to the sitting room where he plays with Ruth. I get down one of the photograph albums for him to look at. The photos are of the Easter-egg hunt earlier in the year. Ruth stands next to him peering at the photographs, her soft, chubby hand resting on his knee.

I am talking to John when I notice that he is not responding. At first I think he's not listening, but then I see that he is opening and closing his mouth like a fish. He lets out a grunt; he tries to talk, but sounds as if he has just come from the dentist. His face seems paralysed.

'I must take you to hospital,' I say.

John shakes his head. His eyes express alarm.

'You don't want to go to hospital?'

He nods and waves his hand, indicating that we should wait.

'Do you want to go home?' I ask.

John nods.

Dick rings Jacques to tell him I'm on my way with John. As I drive through the back streets to Islington, he still manages to show me a short cut which I shall always remember.

When I pull up outside the house, Jacques opens the door and comes down the steps to help him up. He is followed by his partner, David, and another friend Robbie, a doctor.

I drive home, knowing that I have left John in safe hands. But I'm afraid that it may be too late for his plans, that he may have gone beyond that precious moment of decision. Now he may not be capable of killing himself, not without involving someone else and thus causing them to commit a crime. Poor, poor John.

Chapter Six

June–July

The third week of June is a busy time at work. I have lunches, campaign meetings and a radio phone-in to attend. But on Wednesday, I visit John in hospital after work. The faces in the surrounding beds are all different. John has got his speech back. It seems amazing that he has recovered completely from the stroke. He tells me that he suffered another stroke soon after arriving in hospital. This time it was on his other side, but his speech was also affected as on the first occasion. The doctors are very interested, he says, because speech is usually only affected when the left side of the brain is involved. He is weary of the doctors' attention. They want him to have more tests so that they can investigate further, but he is not concerned. He wants to go home tomorrow.

(In retrospect, this information was interesting. My father wondered whether this curious phenomenon was linked in some way to John's dyslexia and early learning difficulties.)

I feel that the doctors are very kind, but they are so much at the frontier of the AIDS research that they view the patients as guinea-pigs. Many of the drugs John is given have ghastly side-effects which he takes other drugs to counteract. It could go on for ever. At some stage you have to decide where the cut-off point is. Is it worth suffering just in order to prolong your life? I know John's answer to that question, and I know that he is coming close to giving it.

John is looking terrible. His skin is oddly pale under the residue of his Greek tan, and he seems anxious. He says that a man in the bed on the opposite side of the room keeps staring at him. I think he is getting paranoid, and am terrified that the virus will affect his brain and cause dementia. But when I look across at the man, I see that he is actually staring at John in a disturbingly menacing way. I pull over the curtain to block him from view, and tell John not to worry.

On 23 June, Dick and I go to 'Sports Pages', the specialist sports bookshop in Charing Cross Road, for the launch of Mike Marqusee's book on cricket and the English establishment, *Anyone But England*. Inside the shop it is crowded and sweaty; we spill out into the street. There are several familiar faces; a lot of old friends are there, including Adam and Robyn Sisman.

Mike's writings about the reactionary world of the cricket establishment have won him few friends among the cricket-loving English, but many of his supporters are there this evening, including the journalist Francis Wheen and MP Peter Hain.

Adam introduces me to Peter Hain and, to my embarrassment, tells him that I was once a student radical. It is true that in my teenage years I spent weekends going on anti-apartheid demonstrations, or writing subversive magazines to distribute around my school along with the *Little Red Schoolbook*. Once I even gave an outraged speech in Hyde Park when Mrs Thatcher, as Minister for Education, scrapped free bus passes for schoolchildren. Afterwards, I was interviewed by the BBC and presented as the voice of 'Kids' Lib'.

Peter Hain looks interested, but I back away. No longer involved with politics, I am not feeling robust enough to defend my position. I spent my first year at Oxford being active in university politics. This was in the mid-1970s, a period of student rebellion, and it was fun. We occupied buildings and marched, chanting slogans, through the streets of Oxford on a regular basis. But I soon became bored with all the cell meetings and disillusioned with the type of people who were attracted to this. The only student politician I really took to was Dave Aaronovitch, who was a fresher at Balliol and in those days a member of the Communist Party. He was remarkably quick-witted and funny, and the most spectacular public speaker I had ever seen. I wheedled my way into his affections and enjoyed his company, and politics, for a few months. However, in spite of being an Exhibitioner, Dave never did a scrap of work while at Oxford and was finally sent down at the end of the second term for failing his history exams.

I was sad to see Dave go but quietly relieved that I could stop being political, for I had decided long ago that the students who most interested me did other things. I retained an intellectual interest in political science – I was studying it, after all – but my experience of student politics had permanently put me off people who love political intrigue and think nothing of stuffing a few ballot boxes when it suits them.

At Mike's party now, I am sorry not to talk to Peter Hain; close-up, he is strikingly sexy. But I am hardly in a fit state for small talk, let alone flirtation. I feel inadequate and fragile. In such a mood, it is safer to stick with old friends.

Saturday, 2 July, at the school fair. Dick cooks the beefburgers, as he does twice a year, while I put the cooked burgers in the buns and take the money. My brain feels so muddled that I keep making mistakes with the change. I must seem like an idiot. The children run around with their friends.

In the evening Dick and I go to Clapham for a dinner party being given by Chris and Vicky Huhne, for Chris' fortieth birthday. The Huhnes' dinner parties are often huge and serious, so we are relieved to find that this is simply dinner for a small group of friends – Con Normanby and his wife Nicky, Patrick Wintour and Madeleine Bunting, and Chris's sister Ella and her husband Piers.

Chris, Con and Patrick were all contemporaries of mine at Oxford. Con and I held a joint twenty-first birthday party at the farmhouse we shared in Farmoor, and later that year I came to know Ella when she and I drove all the way across the United States in an old blue VW beetle we had bought in Boston, and sold to an Iranian student in Eugene, Oregon, for more than we'd paid for it.

It is a wonderfully relaxed evening among old friends. I do not mention John once, and I relish the break.

The following day, Sunday, I take Rebecca and Alice to a press preview of *The Lion King* in Leicester Square. The cinema is packed with journalists with their young children. Usually I would be happy to see someone I know; today I keep my head down. I cannot concentrate on the film and my thoughts drift constantly back to John, imagining how frightening life must be for him.

That evening Adam comes to supper, so frustrated at John and his behaviour that it shocks me. I have to remind myself again that just because people are ill or dying, they don't become different. Just as Oma does not change; in her old age she becomes more of what she really is.

Adam is looking exhausted. He has been holding the New York business together on his own, spending a lot of time with lawyers on the impending lawsuit and trying to be the perfect little brother and son at the same time. He has arrived for a two-week stay and he is furious. Just before he left New York, he received the credit card bill for John and Jacques' holiday in Greece. Somehow they had managed to spend $15,000 in one week. Everything was loaded on to the card, which Adam now has to pay.

I cannot see why he should be so cross. 'But can't it all get paid off with the million-pound pay-out from John's life insurance policy?' Until now I had not questioned John's lifestyle because I assumed that there would be enough at the end to cover all the bills he is running up. Adam's answer makes me shudder.

John originally took out the life insurance policy when he was first diagnosed as HIV in 1986, before insurance companies became fully aware of HIV and its implications. This was also when Adam took out a policy for £1,000,000, and Simon one for £500,000. They were all business partners and wanted some protection in the event of an accident. The younger men wanted Simon to have some cover because they were investing in his new business at that time.

During those glory years, they had paid their premiums without even thinking about it. Then in 1993, when John and Adam were living and working in New York, though in separate apartments, John became seriously depressed. He did not like New York and found it difficult to make friends. A poor judge of character, he was often exploited by people attracted to his wealth and generosity who clearly only wanted to get something out of him without giving anything back.

In the summer of that year, he sank into a deep gloom when he stayed indoors and hardly ever went out. He told Adam that one evening he had come round to his apartment building and stood outside in the street looking up at Adam's window and crying his eyes out. 'You always seem to be surrounded by happy people,' he told him.

Adam persuaded John to see a doctor. 'Suddenly John was feeling okay. A doctor had confirmed that he was depressed, and his mood improved for a while.'

During that period John often came home to London to see Jacques at the house in Alwyne Road. When he was gloomy, Jacques always made him feel better.

It was apparently during that summer of 1993 that John stopped paying the premiums for his life insurance policy. He could no longer see the point in keeping them up. But he never mentioned this to Adam until one day, he said casually, 'I feel bad about the life insurance.'

There was just enough time to pay the back premiums and keep the policy going. But Adam decided not to; he did not want to benefit from John's death.

Adam moans now that he can see that his decision was daft. John has no estate to speak of; his house belongs to the bank, to whom both he and Adam have to pay £10,000 every month for their business debts. In addition, the bank still holds the deeds to Wiblings as collateral. Adam says that the only money due on John's death will be a £40,000 pension pay-out, and that will have to be used to pay off part of his current debts. However, John thinks Jacques should have this £40,000. 'It's very common,' Adam says dryly, 'for dying people to offer the earth to their friends, to buy their help and attention as the end approaches. The problem is, it's not really John's to offer anyone.'

This news makes me furious and exasperated. How irresponsible can John be? And what has Jacques been doing all this time? I know he defers to John on financial matters, but surely he should have thought about safeguarding his position himself?

I keep my thoughts to myself, but I dread the fall-out. John's 'million-pound insurance policy' is famous in the family. Everyone knows about it, and everyone assumes that all and any debts will be covered by it. Now, even the money owed to Mum is not covered. I can imagine Mark and Jane's fury when this fact comes out, but I cannot even begin to imagine what would happen if we lost Wiblings to the bank. I would find that very hard to forgive.

Two days later, on 6 July, a young cousin of Dick's arrives from North Carolina. I originally expected the building work to be finished by the time this girl arrived – but, of course, it's not. It is getting there, slowly, but the builders are not out of our lives.

Before Megan comes, Dick and I are a little concerned. She lives in the Bible belt and is fourteen years old. How on earth will she react to what is going on in our London household? It hardly seems the best time to welcome a young relative, but the trip has been arranged for a long time and she has been looking forward to her stay so much that it would seem selfish to cancel it.

Fortunately, we do not need to worry. Although Megan comes from the American South, her parents are Northern liberals and their daughter shares their views and values. Despite her youth, she seems a mature and sensible girl. However, Dick and I decide not to explain about my brother's condition unless absolutely necessary, as this will give us a break. We know we can manage this as there is no reason why she should even meet John during her stay.

Megan fits into the household easily. She is at that fascinating half-way point between being a child and becoming an adult, quite capable of holding her own in adult conversation but also happy to talk and play with the children. Our girls take to her straight away. Megan has inherited plenty of the family wit and it is interesting to hear her talk about the family with Dick, who is her father's first cousin. She offers to baby-sit for us whenever we want, which proves helpful in the circumstances.

On 7 July, I go with Rachel – deputy editor of *Cosmo*, and a good friend – to Stoke Newington, to the launch party for Kate Figes' book. Kate took over my job on *Cosmo* as fiction editor when I left, and I am fond of her. I have no idea why I am going, but I suspect it is partly out of curiosity to see Kate's house, her children and her husband. I have only ever met her in a professional setting. And her mother, the writer Eva Figes, is there too, relaxed in her role as a grandmother. Normally I would stay longer, but I begin to feel anxious and ill at ease. It is not the sort of large party where you can flit from person to person without getting too involved in conversation. It is a small intimate gathering of serious people, and the only serious subject on my mind at that point is not one I wish to discuss with strangers.

I leave and set off down the streets of Stoke Newington, looking for a taxi to take me home. I drift through the unfamiliar roads and feel as if I'm in a dream, disconnected from everything. I have an intense feeling that the climax is coming. The past six months have been relatively quiet, though the momentum has been building. Now I have a strong sense of foreboding. The last few weeks have brought more serious changes to John's health. The end cannot be far away.

On Monday, 11 July, I go to the London Library in my lunch hour. The moment I leave the office, my thoughts switch to my novel. I have taught myself to avoid thinking about John and put my anxiety about him to fruitful use, as fuel for my writing.

I buy a sandwich in Boots, Piccadilly and, before I go into the hushed atmosphere of the Library, I eat it while sitting on a wooden bench in St James's Square. I have followed this routine for nearly a decade now, throughout every month of the year, unless I have been lunching with a publisher or agent.

It is overcast but hot. Office workers sit on the benches with their lunch-boxes and take-away sandwiches. Couples stretch out and smooch on the grass. Fat, disfigured London pigeons strut about waiting for more crumbs to come their way. Flying rats, Dick always calls them. I wolf down my sandwich and then cross the road to the London Library in the corner. There I sit in the Reading Room on the first floor and enter my imaginary world of Kentish Town in the 1930s. As usual, I write in long-hand in my student Filofax.

The act of writing is soothing. When I re-emerge into the sunlight forty minutes later, I feel completely refreshed. The book has become my escape, my lifeline. I hope briefly that if I am to produce more than one book, I shan't always need something as awful as John's death to spur me on.

Tuesday, 12 July. John and Jacques come to supper, bringing a birthday present for Rebecca who turned eight on Sunday. It is a good age; I remember being eight myself. Notwithstanding the housekeeper, it was a time when life was fun and uncomplicated. I remember John as an eight-year-old too, a skinny child with bony knees sticking out from his grey school shorts, a sweet-natured, shy little boy who was always anxious to say the right thing.

Dick is out with Megan at the theatre on this gloriously warm summer evening. We sit outside on the benches in the garden. The builders have left a lot of their stuff about, so we move the table out on to the lawn, picking our way over the rubble. They have nearly finished, but I wish they would be gone for good. I am truly sick of them. The day before, when I came home from work I noticed a damp patch against the brand-new brick wall at the back. To me this showed that the plumbing had been fixed wrongly, and I had visions of years of rising damp and dry rot ahead of us. I asked Dick to find out from Dave what the problem was with this corner at the back of the house. The simple answer, he learned, was that this was the spot where the builders urinated during the day, out of sight from the neighbours!

I tell John and Jacques this story and we laugh. Then I remember that Dave the builder has not returned the table he took away to be renovated by his friend. I make a mental note to ask about it and get it back.

There is a good atmosphere that evening. John and Jacques are in a light-hearted mood. The children, running around in their pyjamas, are solicitous and keen to find every excuse to stay up beyond bedtime. Dick has left us a cold dinner, all prepared beforehand, so I only have to make the salad.

I have a sudden urge to take some photographs. For some time I have been keen to record John's last months, but felt wary of appearing voyeuristic. Time is running out, particularly as I find it impossible to keep a proper diary to record all the events. Alice begs me to let her take some pictures with my camera. I have not the heart to say no, but I tell her she can take one only. In fact, there is only one frame left; she snaps John and Jacques smiling into the camera. (When the print comes back, I am sad to see that only John's left half is included in the frame. It would have been a wonderful shot; Jacques is smiling. John looks pale and thin but he manages a big smile too.)

Out on our lawn in Kentish Town, we eat Dick's cold chicken and salad. Everything seems quite stable. It is a balmy evening and we relax and laugh a lot. For once we manage to talk about things other than John's health and suddenly again it seems hard to believe that my brother is close to dying.

The next day, however, 13 July, we lurch into a crisis again. After work I go to the school to see Alice's teacher about her end-of-term report. Almost the moment I get home, Jacques telephones; his voice is urgent. He says John was complaining of chest pains in the morning, went to the hospital for a check-up and was immediately admitted again with suspected pneumonia.

Jacques then pauses. 'Emma, I need to talk to you.'

This is the real reason for the urgency in his voice; he wants to see me. 'Can we meet tomorrow after work? In the bar at the Café Royal?'

I check my diary. I am free and agree without hesitation. 'I'll see you at six o'clock.'

Putting down the telephone, I tell Dick that Jacques wants to see me. Talking it over, we cannot be sure what Jacques wants. The more I think about the proposed meeting, the more uneasy I feel. What can it be about? I have no idea whatsoever, but I am aware of the friction between Jacques and Adam over financial arrangements after John's death. I can only hope that Jacques will not try to put me in a difficult position with regard to Adam.

All the next day, I find myself dreading the evening. I have a busy morning, starting with a meeting with the woman from W.H. Smith to discuss the details of the *She*/WHS Children's Book Award we are organising. I also have to do a couple of local radio interviews about features in the current issue. It is difficult to concentrate, and every time I think about the coming evening I feel a sharpness in my throat and a dragging feeling in my chest.

The end of the working day comes. Leaving the office, I walk slowly across Golden Square towards the Café Royal, fearful of what Jacques will have to say. For some reason I think he is going to tell me a dreadful secret about my little brother, something I would rather not know, which will compromise me in some way.

It is not an easy meeting. We sit at a table by a wall and drink white wine. Jacques does not tell me bluntly what he wants, but talks in a roundabout way.

'You know I love John very much,' he begins.

'Yes, I know. You are very good to him. We all love him,' I add. This is not a competition to see who loves my brother the most.

Jacques repeats that he loves John very much, and that he is not interested in any money. I am cautious, since I have never spoken about money to Jacques, and no one has said anything to me. Has someone said something to him? Jacques mentions a £40,000 pension fund from A-Z, which I know will be going to Adam. Adam is a trustee of that fund, so the only way that Jacques could get the money would be if Adam agrees. Does Jacques seriously think that I will get involved in this? Does he expect me to influence Adam?

I say nothing. I am annoyed to be put in this position, but I also feel sad for Jacques who on John's death will lose his home and have to find another place to live. Although he is a successful designer, his earnings (for reasons unknown to me) have never been as high as John's and the two of them have always enjoyed such an extravagant lifestyle. John is still enjoying it as much as he can, up to the very end; for Jacques, it will all end with John's death.

Choosing my words carefully, I gently say that John actually has big debts already. 'He has debts to the family, Jacques, serious debts that have to be paid back with any funds that are available on his death.'

I sense that Jacques is trying to get me on his side in an anticipated bust-up with Adam. John's financial commitments are also Adam's, and Adam too is anxious to repay what is owed to the family.

Jacques looks at me anxiously – hoping, I think, that I will take him under my big-sister wing. Weary and unable to say much, I repeat that John has debts. Jacques still looks at me without appearing to understand. This information is not sinking in; he cannot see it from the family's point of view at all. Perhaps he thinks we owe it to him to provide financial support even when John has died. He thinks we are a rich family that can brush off debts as an inconvenience. Sipping my wine to hide the frown on my face, I silently tell myself not to say what I am thinking, not to tell him how angry I am about the financial mess John is about to leave.

Outside in busy Regent Street, we hug each other goodbye as if we are the closest of friends, then part. As I walk up the road towards the tube, I feel like a hypocrite. I am crumbling inside. Jacques thinks I am on his side and I have not told him otherwise. It is hard enough keeping together for John, and I don't know if I can cope with the impending battle between Jacques and Adam. Little do I know that I shall be hit by the long-term fall-out, too.

The next day, Friday, after work I go yet again to visit John in hospital. It is a sunny evening outside but the ward is stuffy and hot as Dick meets me by John's bedside. John is looking terrible, gaunt and pale. He says he feels nauseous all the time, partly caused by the septrim drip which has been set up to combat the pneumonia. He is also agitated. 'This is it,' he declares. 'I'm going to discharge myself tomorrow. I can't risk going on for any longer. Jacques wants me to wait another week, but I can't.'

'I have to do it fast and before anyone else knows. But I don't want Imogen to know because it could get her into trouble.'

I swallow hard and nod. Another family secret.

John seems excited by having made this decision at last. He pushes himself up on the bed. 'People say there's nothing to fear but the fear, and they're right. And I do believe that there is something after death, some life force or something.'

Dick and I are silent, unable to join him in this discussion about spirituality. It is slightly bizarre to hear him struggling with such serious issues at this point.

John pauses and then continues. I sense that he has rehearsed these words several times. 'I want you both to organise my funeral. I've chosen some music and I'll leave the CDs out on the table for you. I still have to make a final choice. I want you to arrange the funeral because I know that Jacques will be too upset to do it. I don't want any religious stuff.'

We murmur that we shall do whatever he wishes.

There is a silence and then Dick asks brightly, 'Do you want any hymns or songs?'

John looks blankly at him, then he smiles sheepishly. 'I don't know any hymns.'

We look at him and he suddenly remembers. 'Well, I do know "Jerusalem". Would that be all right?' He looks anxious, unsure whether his suggestion is appropriate.

'You can have anything you want,' I say.

'Okay, "Jerusalem" then,' he agrees with a little shrug.

We nod and smile. It's all settled, then; we don't try to change his mind. I too think he should do it soon if he is going to succeed. I sit in the chair by his bed, staring at the patterns on the worn cotton cover which seem to float about before my eyes. I am aware of the nurses moving around in the ward near us. Everything seems to have speeded up all of a sudden. There's no stopping it now. I can tell by John's manner that he means it, he cannot stop and wait or it will be too late.

'Will you say goodbye before you do it? I'd like you to do that, John,' I say tentatively.

He shakes his head. 'No, it's better if no one knows about it. No goodbyes are best.'

There is silence again. I feel rejected.

John takes a deep breath and speaks again, his voice cracking. 'And speaking of Jacques, I want him to be looked after,' he says. 'He's been very good to me and I want him looked after.'

'Yes,' I murmur again and I say nothing. Inside I can feel a great rage surfacing. I am angry and shouting silently at him: 'Who is going to look after Jacques, and with what? Here you are with some romantic idea that your death-bed wish will make it come about. How dare you make promises to Jacques that you're not in a position to make? How dare you give him unrealistic expectations and leave the rest of us to sort out the mess when you've gone? You have no money to grant favours!'

But one doesn't shout at a dying man, even if he deserves it.

I say nothing. I give him a kiss and say I'll call him the next day.

It is impossible to believe that this is the last time I will ever see him. 'I'll speak to you tomorrow.'

Dick and I sit on the tube home without saying a word.

At home, the children are lively and I join in their games, trying to forget what is about to happen. The girls have not mentioned John for quite a while. He has not died and I think they may have forgotten that he is ill.

After a fretful night, I get up and telephone John at the hospital. It is about 10 o'clock on a warm, sunny morning. 'I've just discharged myself,' he says. 'Paul is here and I'm about to leave. Jacques will ring you when my body is found.'

It seems surreal. This is it. 'I love you, Johnny,' I shout down the phone, my voice cracking. Then I put down the receiver and burst into tears. John's death has begun.

Dick and I spend the day with the girls, unable to talk about what is on our minds. I play and smile and laugh, but underneath I feel unbearably sad. Megan is still with us. She is fun and good with the children, who seem particularly lively and joyful that day. She agrees to baby-sit while Dick and I go out for a meal that evening.

We walk over to Primrose Hill, to a restaurant called Big Night Out. We sit upstairs. It is noisy and smoky, and the food isn't particularly exciting. We drink a ridiculous amount of wine and say little. All the time I keep thinking: 'My little brother is killing himself at this very moment.' I imagine him swallowing the pills. I think about Agatha Christie's book *Ten Little Niggers*, and wonder who will be the next of us to go. First Simon, then John. Then who? I think about the family photographs my mother took of us in the early 1960s – the splendid family of six healthy children in the garden of our old Dulwich home. That fantasy has been shattered. I try not to imagine what my mother feels because it hurts too much when I do.

We stagger home and fall into bed, dreading the next day.

PART TWO

Dying Again

Chapter Seven

Sunday, 17 July

The next day we wake up with heavy hangovers. The children's cheerfulness at breakfast is painful as we sit outside round the table. They tell scatological jokes and giggle into their Rice Krispies. Ruth leans back in her high chair and swigs milk from her bottle. She is rather old to be drinking from a bottle still, but she looks so cute doing it that we shall indulge her for a few months more. Besides, I don't feel strong enough to start battling with her yet. She is wedded to that bottle.

In spite of my hangover, I have an urge to get out of the house and surround myself with life. We decide to take Megan down to have dim sum in Chinatown and then to Covent Garden to see the performers. This is a favourite Sunday outing with the children and they are delighted. They skip down the road and play I-Spy on the tube.

In the Chinese restaurant we eat pork dumplings and fried squid, chickens' feet and fat white noodles. The children pick and choose. As usual, Alice is the most adventurous and tucks into the chickens' feet with greedy relish. After lunch we wander down Long Acre into Covent Garden where the performers are in full swing. A booth in the far corner attracts the girls' attention and they sit on the cobblestones with the other children to watch their first performance of a Punch and Judy show. I am pleased to see that it's not a sanitised version; Mr Punch is vicious to his wife and then gets his comeuppance from the policeman. When a volunteer is requested, Ruth sticks up her hand without hesitation and joins in, holding the sausages which she then won't return. She's a performer, our little Ruth. The crowd clap her and she wants to perform some more.

Later as we head back home, my legs feel heavy. I am dreading the next few hours. Dick and I hardly speak to each other, our thoughts elsewhere.

When we get in at about 6 p.m., the answer machine indicates that there is a message. I turn it on, expecting it to be Jacques, but it's the cheerful voice of a friend wanting to arrange lunch the following week. I don't ring back. I'll do it later, or tomorrow, I decide.

We give the children tea. At about 7 o'clock, the telephone rings; this time it is Jacques.

'He's dead, isn't he?' I say flatly.

Jacques sounds in despair. 'No, he's not! I've just come in and he just looks as if he's in a deep sleep. He's breathing very heavily; he's snoring.'

Muddled thoughts flash through my head. Do people snore when they are dying? Perhaps it's the death rattle, whatever that is. When people die of an overdose of sleeping pills, do they just sink into a deeper and deeper sleep until everything stops? I feel angry at my ignorance. Why don't I know the answers to these questions?

'Perhaps you have to wait a little longer,' I suggest. 'But you should not be there, Jacques.'

I know that if he does not act – either leave or call the doctor – he could be in trouble. It's illegal to assist in a suicide, even passively.

Jacques sounds bewildered and panicked. 'He took the pills nearly twenty-four hours ago. They should have worked by now.' Then he says he has to go but he'll call me again later.

It seems like a nightmare. I have been imagining John is dead while in fact he was sleeping in bed. He was snoring, for heaven's sake!

As I put down the telephone, it rings again. I snatch it up and am surprised to hear David Jockelson calling to ask how things are going. David is a solicitor whose children are at the same school as mine. He often gives me a lift into town in his car on his way to his office, so we have had some pretty open conversations about our respective families. David has followed the John saga with interest and genuine concern, and he knows that matters are reaching a climax.

'Well, as we speak,' I say, 'I am waiting for a call to tell me that John's dead. He's taken a whole lot of sleeping pills. It'll be over by the time I see you tomorrow.' I cannot bring myself to tell him that in fact John is snoring.

David apologises for holding up the phone at such a crucial time and rings off.

I quickly relay the news to Dick as we bath the children and put them to bed. With Megan around it is difficult to talk freely, so it is obviously time to fill her in on the situation. As we sit in the garden eating our supper in the evening light, we tell her about John's HIV and about his suicide attempt.

Megan takes it all in with characteristic calmness. She is sympathetic and expresses her sadness for John; she does not seem to be afraid of AIDS or disgusted by homosexuality. Her calm acceptance of the situation would be admirable in anyone; in a fourteen-year-old, it's astonishing.

The telephone rings and we all jump. It is not Jacques, but another friend. I say I will call back.

I ring Jacques, hoping that this time it *has* happened, that the pills have finally done their job. But it is not to be. When he answers, I can hear other people talking in the background. 'He's surfacing,' Jacques says. 'He's waking up. He's moving around now and moaning. But Imo's here, also Paul and David.'

I am immediately relieved to know that Imo is there – Imogen the doctor, the family friend. Not only will she have taken charge but her presence now means that Jacques and the other boys will not be in danger of being accessories, or whatever one is to a suicide.

After the build-up, I am ashamed to find myself almost disappointed. I have been gearing myself up for this death, and it has not happened. All that imagining was for nothing. In some weird way I feel as though I've been wasting my time. We have lived through John's death, and now we will have to go through it again when it finally does happen.

But my selfish thoughts are swamped by my feelings for poor John when I imagine what he will feel like when he finally regains consciousness. What ultimate horror, to say goodbye to the world and then fail. All that courage wasted!

Dick and I decide that we must go over to Canonbury immediately. Megan agrees to baby-sit.

It is getting dark as the cab takes us to Islington. On the way Dick and I agree with exasperation that it is typical of John to botch his suicide. Why on earth did he not do it properly and put a plastic bag over his head? Now, who knows what the repercussions will be? This is a mess, the

clockwise from top: Mark, Simon, John, Adam, Emma, Jane. Dulwich, 1963.

John aged two. London, 1961.

John with Adam and our mother. Germany, 1968.

John at the Gatehouse School. London, 1969.

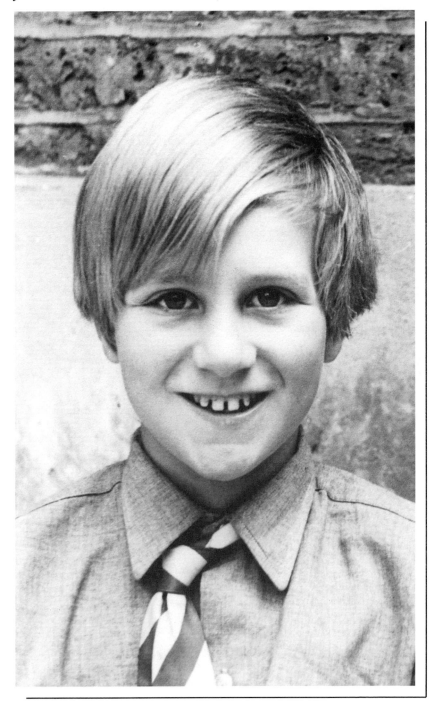

John and his cat, Humphrey. Sussex, 1984.

Adam and John with their fleet of A–Z bikes. London, 1986.

John and Ruth at Falkland Road, 1993.

We all admire Tsar, the new kitten. Alwyne Road, April 1994.

Oma's 90th birthday party: Oma, Peter and John. Sussex, April 1994.

Alice's last shot of John and Jacques. Falkland Road, July 1994.

worst possible scenario. My feelings swing from rage to pity and back again.

It is about 10 o'clock when we arrive at the house. David opens the door; he looks grave. 'They're all upstairs,' he says, always aware and respectful of everyone's grief. His tolerance of the situation and of Jacques' devotion to John always amazes me. Most people would be insanely jealous; but never the saintly David, always sensible and sensitive to others.

'You can go up,' he says. He stays downstairs.

We hurry up to the next floor and walk into the large bedroom which looks over the street. A side light casts a warm yellow glow across the scene. On the table by the wall is a row of candles that have burned down completely. Imogen, standing by John's bed and feeling his pulse, looks up and smiles a welcome. Jacques and Paul stand on either side, watching John who is naked apart from a pair of underpants. His suntan shows up clearly against the rumpled white sheets.

John is lying flat, breathing heavily and noisily through his mouth. Occasionally he moans and moves a leg or an arm. The noise is both alarming and embarrassing. We stare at him in horror. What is he going to feel when he wakes up?

Imogen says that she has checked him over and, as far as she can tell, no damage has been caused. The three of them tell us how Paul and Jacques had decided quite soon to call Imogen, as John's GP.

When she arrived they denied that John had taken anything, claiming that they had just found him like this. But she suspected that John had taken something and telephoned the hospital. It was evident that he was surfacing and she discussed the situation with the hospital consultant and told him that she would stay the night to check that he is all right.

We stand in that darkened room and wait. There is nothing

else to do except watch John gradually come round from the deep drug-induced sleep. His breathing becomes more varied. Occasionally he lets out a loud snort, the kind of noise that makes children giggle at sleeping adults or irritated spouses nudge the other in bed or at the theatre. But there is no giggling now.

We can only look on, impotent and appalled, as John slowly comes to life again. His legs move more frequently. He bends one leg at the knee and drops it down again. He grimaces and strains, as though he is struggling to climb out of that long sleeping body of his and emerge into the world of light once more.

It is nearly midnight and we have to work the next day. John still is not conscious when Dick and I finally leave. I am reluctant to go, but it could be hours before he actually wakes up.

Imogen confirms that she will stay and watch John through the night. There is another bed in the room; she will sleep in that. I ask her to telephone if there is any significant change. As we go, I notice the CDs on the table in the sitting room – left there by John. There is no note or anything. I suppose he felt he had said goodbye and there was nothing more to say. John was never big on words, except when he was stoned or drunk. But I am disappointed that there is no extra message for me.

Then I chide myself for thinking that he had any special feelings for me. I know that in fact he is closer to Jane and always has been. They were nearer in age and I was the maternal but bossy older sister, the one who could be counted on to get things done when necessary but who did not join in with the naughty pranks they got up to as children. I understand the way it is, but it still stings me.

'He didn't leave a message for anyone,' Dick says quietly, reading my thoughts.

We scoop up the CDs and leave.

First thing the next morning, I telephone, relieved not to have had a call during the night. Imogen answers; she says that John is now conscious and aware of what has happened, that he is extremely distressed to discover that he is still alive. She is talking him through it all now and telling him how things will be managed from now on.

Imogen has also asked me to pass the news on to my mother, so I ring her in Sussex straight away. Standing by the window, I watch a squirrel move in jerky bounces across the road. The children are romping around the kitchen and provide a noisy background for the news. My mother is appalled. John telephoned her to say goodbye two days ago, so she has been waiting to hear that he is dead.

I can hear the panic in her voice. 'Oh, my God! Has he got brain damage?'

'Imogen says he's all right, there's no damage.'

I am just as relieved by that information myself. My mother has always warned us of the dangers of suicide attempts, and of the terrible damage that can arise from a bungled effort – the stomach bleeding caused by aspirins, the liver failure of para-cetamol, the brain damage, the paralysed limbs.

I always lapped up the details my mother recounted of her experiences as a young doctor when having to deal with suicide attempts that failed, and I have always known that the appar-ently easy ways to do it are fraught with particular dangers. Anyone wanting to know how John's situation could be any worse has only to imagine him living the rest of his life (how-ever long that is) in a coma, or dying in agony from internal bleeding or liver damage.

My mother used to talk about the dangers but then, as I grew older, I would hear of real examples. Dick has a friend who tried to commit suicide by taking an overdose but woke up hours later with a permanently paralysed arm because she had lain on it and cut off the blood supply. We also know of someone who tried to kill herself by jumping out of the window. She ended up as a paraplegic and will spend the rest of her life in a wheelchair.

That's how life can be even worse. At least John has not harmed himself, so far as we know. That really is looking on the bright side . . .

My mother says she will ring Imogen and Peter. I hang up and get the children ready for school and myself for work. I have meetings and radio interviews in the morning, which I cannot miss.

I am honest with the girls and I tell them what has happened; there is no point in trying to conceal it from them. They pick up everything that is said and read every expression on adult faces.

Rebecca and Alice stare at me shocked and wide-eyed. It seems so sudden. When they saw John just a few days ago, he looked fine. What prompted him to make such a decision? How can it all suddenly change? They don't understand how anyone can try to kill themselves, let alone fail. They do know that their Uncle Simon killed himself, but that was with a gun, and they are aware that guns kill people. I try to explain about this thing we all call 'quality of life' and how the value some people place on that can be stronger than what we all refer to as the 'will to live'. It's way above their heads, I can see that, but as I gather up their school folders and recorders and count out the dinner money, I cannot think of a simpler way to say it. How can these little girls understand the sadness of adults? How can they understand that things can be so bad for some people that they are prepared to leave behind those they love?

I take Rebecca and Alice to school, leaving Ruth with Dick. Anne will be arriving at 9.30.

At the school I barely see anyone. I am in a rush and race past the other parents. I am often offered a lift into the West End by David Jockelson, who had telephoned the day before. As I come up to the car he asks me what has happened. As I open my mouth to answer, another mother who also works in the West End comes up and asks for a lift.

'He failed,' I hiss at David. 'It didn't work. He's woken up.'

David looks aghast and we climb into the car; then another regular passenger joins us. I am desperate to talk to David about John's failed suicide, but not with the other people there.

I sit silently in the front seat as the others chat gaily about their weekends. When asked what I did, I merely mention our dinner at Big Night Out and going to Covent Garden. It sounds uneventful, as weekends go.

At work, I tell Linda what has happened and she is immediately sympathetic; I must do what's necessary, she says. Even without her explicit permission, I now know what I have to do. For months I have been juggling work and family responsibilities, trying to keep my job going as if nothing were happening outside the office, as if I weren't trying to bring up three children and run a house (albeit with a husband who behaves like an adult) and also do my bit for a dying brother.

If the situation involved my own child, I know that I would have given in earlier. Perhaps if it were a parent, I would have given in sooner too. The fact that John is a sibling, and one of many, made me hold out as though I felt I did not have the right to take time away from work for him. It had nothing to do with any pressure or the attitudes of my colleagues at work – solely to do with what was in my own head.

Anyway, now there is no doubt about what must be done. I am still worried about work, but Jan Boxshall is my saviour.

Fortunately, Jan has been promoted to managing editor. She comes from *Cosmo*, where we were colleagues. Calm and sensible, she tells me not to worry, that she will take on any of my urgent work. I am so grateful to her.

As I am leaving at lunch-time to see John, one of the sub-editors overhears me say I am going to visit my brother in hospital.

'Is he ill?' she asks, more as a formality than anything else, I guess.

'Yes,' I say bluntly. 'He's dying.'

I sweep from the office leaving the sub looking shocked and embarrassed.

It is unkind of me to make her feel tactless; it is not her fault, but I cannot help myself. I am feeling so angry that I have no room for niceties. Perhaps subconsciously I wanted to make a dramatic scene, to bring real life into the world of our women's magazine where our role is to produce a treat for the readers each month, not make them feel unhappy or guilty.

I make my way to John's house on the route I shall get to know well, taking the Victoria Line to Highbury & Islington, and then walking across the roundabout and up through Canonbury Square with its elegant Georgian terraced houses.

My mother had a flat in this square in the late 1940s, when she was a medical student. My father lived there with her, but would always move out when my grandparents visited so as to maintain a pretence of middle-class respectability and prevent a family row. It seems an amazing coincidence that John should be spending his last days just around the corner from this spot where our parents lived so many years ago before they were married, before even Simon was born. I cannot imagine what thoughts will pass through my parents' heads when they drive through here to visit their son.

Jacques and Paul are in the house when I arrive. Tired and pale, they tell me about the night, about John waking up and his slow horror as he realised what had happened.

My father has driven up from Sussex and just arrived. As he climbs the stairs to see John, I wait behind and talk to Jacques and Paul.

Fifteen minutes later Peter comes down the stairs. He has to leave, and I walk him to the front door.

'He's waiting for the terminal consultant now,' Peter tells me. 'He's expected later today.'

The 'terminal consultant'. That's what doctors used to call the man who sees people through to the end. It's too blunt for today's tastes, so the politically correct title nowadays is palliative care doctor.

Imogen is back at work in her surgery nearby and will be returning in the afternoon when the palliative care team arrives. John did not know about this North London team of doctors and nurses dedicated to seeing that people have 'good deaths'. His greatest fear was of having to go back to hospital, dying there and being wheeled out on a trolley like so many of the fellow patients he had met in that ward. Now we know that it does not have to be like this, that John can be cared for at home, with Imogen as his GP working with the team to ensure that his last days are as comfortable as possible. Knowing this seems like an immense relief. No more trekking to the hospital. No more wards and antiseptic smells. No other dying people to watch and wonder about. Only John to concentrate on.

However, such a plan also requires a lot of care. Jacques cannot do it all himself, and we have to work out a rota so that there is always at least someone at the house ready to answer the door, take telephone calls, bring food and drink up to John. We draw up a schedule and Jacques, Paul and I write in our names for different times on various days of the week. Later, others will also add themselves to the list.

Now it is time to see John. I climb back up the stairs and walk into the bedroom I was in only fifteen hours before. Now it is bright and light. John is sitting up against a lot of pillows. He looks terrible. His hair is awry and greasy looking, his skin is grey. As I bend down to kiss him on the cheek, I can see tears glistening in his eyes.

'Imo is so kind,' he murmurs. 'She's such a good friend. I made a terrible mess, and she cleaned it all up for me. Not many people would have done that.'

I sit next to John, handing him a mug of water to wet his parched lips. He tells me what's going to happen now.

'I shall be given a big injection of morphine and put into a deep sleep until I don't wake up.' He seems relieved, even relaxed, in spite of the weekend's ordeal. Now he is on the right track, he thinks; now he's going to die as he wants. He believes he'll be put out of his misery by being put down like an animal. He has got it all wrong, but I say nothing.

When he gets up to pee he is unsteady on his feet, but manages to negotiate the room and make his way to the bathroom next door. His six-foot-three frame is frail and bent. He is not wearing his pyjama top, and from behind I see his ribs and backbone clearly defined under his skin.

My mother and stepfather arrive from Sussex. They look terrible, worried and tired. I deliberately avoid imagining what it must be like to lose a child. If I let myself even think about the possibility of losing Rebecca or Alice or Ruth, I feel sick.

There's nothing to say. We all have our own personal grief,

so there's no point in trying to comfort anyone else. No one has the right to more comfort or sympathy than the rest.

It is their turn at John's bedside now, and they climb the stairs wearily.

Another friend arrives, Robbie, then finally Dr Rob George and his palliative care team.

Rob is a big, impressive man with a charismatic air. He walks around the room asking people who they are, as if he needs to assess the situation and everyone's relationship with John. Learning that I am family, he gives me a big bear-hug. He shakes hands with others, and hugs Jacques. Then he and his team disappear upstairs to see John.

The doctors and nurses are upstairs for quite a while. Then they come down again and Rob sits with us, anxious to talk about what is to happen.

'I have told John that I am not in the business of killing people . . .' he begins.

I think of poor Johnny expecting, hoping, to be 'put to sleep'. Obviously he is to be disappointed.

'I am interested in giving people a good death,' continues Rob, almost with a missionary zeal.

My mother talks to him, doctor to doctor, but there's not much she can glean from him that we have not already learned.

I go home to see the children and put them to bed. Dick cooks a pile of marinated chicken legs to feed everyone when we return that evening. Megan will baby-sit. We arrive back in a cab, bearing trays of food.

That evening there is quite a gathering at Alwyne Road. Imogen is back. Paul is there with his girlfriend, Ruthie; Robbie, Jacques and David too. We take it in turns to be with John when he is not sleeping.

Dick is pleased that John expresses an interest in the food.

He puts the meat and vegetables on a plate and takes it up himself. When the plate comes down again, the meal has hardly been touched.

We eat and drink and talk, all bound together in this mission. Imogen talks about her night spent sleeping in the other bed in John's room.

'It was like being back together in the dorms at school,' she says. 'With Paul here, too, it was just like the old days.' She is fun and joins in the conversation and laughter, but at regular intervals she becomes the quiet professional and disappears upstairs to monitor John.

We go home late and the children are fast asleep. As I sit by Ruth's cot and watch her sleeping peacefully, I have a memory of John as a little baby. I remember when he was born. I was six and Peter took the rest of us to visit our mother in hospital. She was in a private room; as a doctor, she had privileges. John's was a precipitous birth, arriving as Mum was eating her lunch and a few minutes after the midwife had told her that she was definitely not in labour!

I remember being in the hospital room and staring at this big blond baby in the cot by my mother's bed. He was fast asleep. breathing through puckered lips. I can recall gazing at him and trying to remember whether or not human babies opened their eyes at birth. I knew that puppies and kittens did not, but I did not dare ask for fear of appearing stupid.

My mother read my mind. 'His eyes do open,' she said, smiling. 'He's just asleep, that's all. He's got blue eyes, like all babies.'

John kept his big blue eyes. He and Mark were the blonds in the family; Simon and Jane were the dark ones. Adam was doe-eyed and darkish, I was just mousy. Poor John, his looks have been so important to him all his life. They are all gone now.

My mind is buzzing and I know I shan't be able to get to sleep. I get out the CDs John has left and lie on my back on the sitting-room floor as I listen to his choice of music for his funeral. Now it is unbearable as I let my imagination free and try to place myself in John's body over the past few months while he listened to this in order to decide what would be suitable. It seems to me the saddest thing in the world. I can imagine John sitting with tears in his eyes, caressing his beautiful blue-grey cat as he visualises his own funeral with this music soaring round him over the heads of the mourners.

He has chosen some music by the Gypsy Kings, a mournful wail about the pain of lost love; 'Father and Son', by Cat Stevens, which I find deeply embarrassing now but have to admit I rather liked during my own university days; and the 'Jesu Domine' from Mozart's *Requiem*. I wonder how John came to choose these particular works.

How *do* you choose music for your own funeral? I find myself wondering what I would choose, and I even consider whether it would make a good radio programme – Funeral Tunes instead of Desert Island Discs. Once, on *She*, I commissioned Ian Hislop to write his own obituary, but that was for fun.

Chapter Eight

18–30 July

Over the next few weeks, life takes on a new pace. Equipment, medication and unfamiliar medical accessories are delivered to the house by the NHS. A small fridge for storing all the drugs is installed in the corner by John's bed. Huge stacks of what look like giant nappies, for placing on the bed under him, fill up one side of the wardrobe. There are boxes and boxes of objects in sterilised sealed packets waiting for their one-time use before being disposed of in bright yellow plastic bags which are then picked up by a special NHS collection whenever necessary.

We take turns spending time at the house. Imogen is thinking about John's comfort and suggests buying a garden chair so that he can sit outside in the garden. Despite a move to go to the local Homebase, Jacques and Paul set off in Paul's open sports car to John Lewis and return with a swanky teak sunbed sticking up in the back, complete with well-padded cushions and an attachable tray for drinks. We wince at the £400 price tag.

This incident also raises the painful questions that are to recur throughout the next few weeks. Whose house is it anyway? John and Jacques 'own' it, though they have defaulted on the mortgage. John and Jacques are no longer a couple, so who makes the final decisions about John's care? We are sensitive to Jacques' relationship with John, but I feel that he is less sensitive to the other people in my brother's life. For most of the time Jacques makes the decisions, such as what kind of garden furniture should be bought for John to sit on, where his bed should be positioned in the room. Imogen and I think the bed should be moved around so that John can look out of the window and see the leaves on the trees outside blowing in the wind instead of facing the bedroom door. Jacques agrees, but never gets around to doing it. We don't like to move the bed ourselves because it is Jacques' home.

There are more pressing issues, however, about the amount of diamorphine John ought to be getting and what food he should be eating. Diamorphine is heroin. Most of us feel that Johnny should spend the rest of his days in a sleepy drugged-out state so that he is relaxed and not panicked. Jacques is utterly opposed to this point of view because he wants to stay in contact with John. He wants to communicate with him and have John communicate in return. So it is at Jacques' request that John has enough to keep him calm for some but not all of the time.

The next ten days, until the end of July, settle down to their own pace. John has cheered up and is in relatively good spirits. He comes downstairs for some hours of the day and, when the weather is fine, lies on the sunbed in the pretty back garden. He is now on a permanent dose of diamorphine, enough to keep his spirits up. Imogen adjusts the quantity regularly.

The drug has strange and unexpected side-effects. One afternoon as Robbie and I sit with him in the garden, John is distracted. 'Did you see a fox run across the lawn just then?' he suddenly asks. He is hallucinating.

A few minutes later, he struggles to his feet. 'I'm going to be sick,' he mutters and walks towards a pile of wood in the corner. As he leans over and a jet of vomit spews out of his mouth, he staggers and nearly falls. Luckily, Robbie anticipates the fall and grabs him just in time. John is so tall and gangly that it is hard for him to keep his balance.

The action is now all at the house. Friends and family come to visit. People are respectful of others' time with John, withdrawing from the bedroom to allow newcomers to have their words alone with him.

This is noticeably different from conditions in the hospital when we feel almost a jealous rage if we arrive to find someone else at the bedside, or if somebody comes to visit just when we are about to have a significant conversation. It is a bit like trying to play tennis on a public court where there is no booking system. At least when someone is dying at home, one can wait one's turn patiently in another part of the house and seek company with other visitors.

The feeling of camaraderie is strong. We are all linked by the common sense of purpose arising from being actively involved in someone's death. We see each other frequently. We offer to run errands – walk down to the corner chemist to pick up a prescription of diamorphine for Imogen, drive to Islington to stock up the kitchen with food, make cups of tea for whoever is there.

This is on the surface, at any rate, and it is real. But all the while the tensions are building up, ready to burst into the open at the first opportunity.

For the first few days John spends some hours lying in the garden on the new garden seat. But after a week he is coming downstairs less and less. One night he is carried down for a barbecue with a lot of friends. He is eating very little; his lips are parched and peeling.

On 25 July I arrive at lunch-time and find John up and dressed and ready to go to the hospital with Imogen for a check-up on his eyes. We use the taxi provided by the Council. The eye clinic is crowded and full of old people. John looks so thin and ill; at one point he gets up, staggers and almost loses his footing. I see the old ladies frowning and moving away from him with fear and disapproval.

'Is he drunk?' one of them hisses at another.

I feel like hissing back at her but I keep quiet.

The eye specialist is a serious, gentle woman who must see hundreds of frightened young men like John. She looks into his eyes and says that the right eye is not worse and the left eye seems okay too.

Although cytomegalovirus retinitis is serious and usually progresses until finally it causes loss of vision, the doctor's news suggests that his eyesight will see John out. It would be appalling if he were to go blind before he finally dies.

Back we go in the taxi and put John to bed. He is exhausted. It is like having a toddler again, except that he is so enormous it is hard to manoeuvre him across the room. He thanks people constantly. Always grateful to everyone for their help and concern, he takes none of it for granted. In that sense he is not like a baby but in every other way he is. John has always retained an element of childishness even as a grown man.

Imogen goes back to her other patients at the surgery. The palliative care team visits; I do some work downstairs while they talk to John. Gradually the house fills up again. Jacques comes back from his workshop; he is managing to keep working to some extent through all this. Paul comes over, as does Robbie. Rob George comes down the stairs and sits with us. He wants to know how Jacques is. The set-up must be a little confusing for him but he does not show it. He talks about John and how he has been a bit upset, but he has now left him imagining himself by a doorway.

This odd remark prompts Jacques to put the question we all want to ask. 'What happens if, like John, you don't believe in God?'

Rob is unfazed. He has been asked this many times before. 'Every family or group has something it believes in. That is what counts, and matters. I've told John that there is a "Here" and a "There". Everyone has their own way of getting to "There". Some people find it through religion, others have different means.'

Nobody says anything. It sounds a bit wishy-washy and not a satisfactory answer to me. As a family we were not brought up with a faith in anything. John has nothing to hang on to except whatever he makes up now. It would be so much easier to believe in a God and afterlife. If you believe in heaven and you think that's where you're headed, that's fine. It must be very comforting. I can understand why some people become religious as they get older and return to the faith of their childhood when they come close to death.

The trouble is, even if there were a heaven I'm not sure that John would be going there, after the way he's behaved over Simon's will and all the debts. But I keep my thoughts to myself. It is a terrible thing to think, and I don't even make a joke about it.

However, jokes do fly about, providing comforting relief during those days. One evening Dick and I are sitting with

John when he suddenly remembers that as he was about to climb the stairs for what he thought was the last time, just before he took the pills, his therapist telephoned to ask why he had not been to see him for a while.

We laugh out loud. It seems like a joke out of a Woody Allen film. Dick tells the Woody Allen line: 'My analyst is a strict Freudian. You have to keep paying for the sessions even if you commit suicide.'

We chuckle again and I imagine adding John's therapist to that inevitable list of creditors when he dies. Perhaps it is good that he expects payment each time, that man. It keeps things clearer all round.

Another thing about these days with John is the chance to spend time with a group of primarily gay men. They are camp and open about their sexual interests and attractions. They all look fit, as they take good care of themselves. It is so different from being with heterosexual men, and the sexual tension that exists between them is unconnected to any woman in the room. Yet I also feel self-conscious. Many of their icons are beautiful women. Jacques is used to dressing beautiful women. He designs clothes for the Princess of Wales. When I think about it I feel like a lump myself, but I remind myself that even my sister-in-law, Clare, who is naturally slim, said she felt like that when she once borrowed an Azagury dress for some posh function.

Most of all, as I listen to them talking about what they do when they're not working, I am struck by how free they are. They stay up late, sleep late, eat out a lot, go to the cinema. Theirs is a life without children, without the domestic ties and obligations that most of us get caught up in at this time of our lives. For me, so bogged down with schools, school lunches and birthday parties, it is hard to imagine what it must be like to be so unattached. It's attractive. On the other hand, what they don't have is the laughter and charm of children, and the sense of time moving on, something that all children bring with them.

On 23 July we say goodbye to Megan, who returns to North Carolina, and I take the children down to Sussex in the car. It is hot and I long to escape from the heat of the city and the pressure of visiting John. Dick stays in London to catch up on all the work he has missed with his stints at Alwyne Road, and the space in the car is taken up by my writer friend Margaret Walters, who is also Alice's godmother even though Alice is not christened.

I have known Margaret for many years, since I edited her first book, *The Nude Male*, in my first job as a book editor. She used to be married to the American writer Clancy Sigal and it was Clancy who – when I would regale him and Margaret with the latest dramatic tales from the Dally household – told me I should be writing novels using the material I had from my family life. It took me many years to see that, but he was right.

Margaret and Clancy have split up, but she remains a good and loyal friend. She has seen plenty of my family and must have first known John when he was a teenager. I still admire the way she laughed when, newly back from Australia, John dismissed the country before the assembled guests at a Thanksgiving dinner with the comment: 'They're all a bunch of criminals, anyway.' His blushes and apologies when informed that Margaret is Australian were charming, but I somehow doubt that he ever learned not to make uninformed comments in the company of people he does not know very well.

The weather is hot and we manage to have a good time. My mother is pleased to have an interesting visitor to stay and help keep the conversation off depressing matters, and we spend an afternoon at a craft festival in nearby Petworth Park. It is such a relief to be distracted from what else is going on.

Once back in London, however, the pressure instantly returns. It is even worse now. The date is 25 July and we have barely a week before we are supposed to go to France. I booked this holiday at the end of last year before we knew anything about John's illness. We are due to leave that Friday and I feel that we need a holiday and a break from London. There is no guarantee that John will die within the next few weeks, so there is no point in cancelling. It is only to Normandy, across the water, so we are not far away if we do have to return urgently.

Those days are frenetic. At the office I am trying to get everything sorted out so that there are no hitches while I am away. This means concentrating and writing detailed notes for Jan about all the work in progress. At least the children have broken up from school so we do not have that early-morning madness, but I feel as if I am in a constant state of frenzy. I dash to the office and somehow get through the day, spending my lunch hours buying things for the holiday. After work I rush up to Alwyne Road to visit John before going home to Kentish Town to have some time with the girls before they go to bed.

Also that week, Barbara Cook is in town and Dick has bought tickets to see her. We cannot miss this. Barbara is the greatest American singer in popular music and we go to see her whenever we can. Her stunning voice invariably brings tears to the eyes.

The first time we saw her was at the Donmar Warehouse in July 1986, then I was heavily pregnant with Rebecca and we sat in the front row. Now we have two treasured tickets to hear Barbara yet again and lose ourselves in the sound of that voice. We visit John first and then go on down the road to Sadler's Wells. It is another steamy evening and the idea of spending it in a hot dark theatre is not enticing. But Barbara Cook is rarely in town, so there's no question of not going. Like many female singers, she is a gay icon, and many in the audience are gay men.

The air-conditioning is not very effective and the theatre is stifling. Even so, the music is wonderfully soothing. Barbara Cook sounds like an angel and I sit entranced. It is the first time I have relaxed for weeks, and I find myself in floods of tears at the beauty of the music, the purity of her voice and the poignancy of some of the songs about love and loss. One in particular tells of someone losing a lover to AIDS: 'Love Don't Need a Reason'. I wonder how many people in the audience are HIV or have AIDS. There are many eyes glistening with tears as she sings, 'Love is all we have for now . . . What we don't have is time . . . Love is never a crime and I just want to stay with you until the end.'

It is an extraordinary evening, both exhilarating and exhausting, and one that will live in my memory for ever.

As we stream out into the warm night air, I feel as though I have been momentarily purged and emotionally fed. It is a weird moment of great happiness, but I am also drained. I am so glad that we are about to escape for two weeks, to get away from everything and just be by ourselves with the children.

Two days later, 28 July, is the day before we go on holiday. When I arrive at the house to take over from Paul, who is going off to work, he tells me the home help is due any minute – this is Maurice, who is provided by the Council and about whom John and Jacques have complained several times.

Maurice arrives twenty minutes later. He stands on the doorstep and then, without a smile, he walks past me into the house. I take a dislike to him immediately.

'What should I do?' he asks.

I peer into the small galley kitchen. 'Well, you could clear up in the kitchen. Do whatever needs doing. There are a few dirty plates in the sink and the sideboard needs wiping and tidying up.'

Maurice frowns. 'I'm not really a cleaner, you know,' he says, thrusting his chin in the air.

I am taken aback. 'What are you, then?'

He looks down at me and shrugs. 'I'm lots of things,' he tells me. 'I'm a companion and a teacher and a counsellor.' He looks into the kitchen which admittedly is relatively tidy, with just a few dirty plates from Jacques' dinner.

'I'm not here to clean up after other people,' he maintains.

Taking a deep breath, I try to keep my temper. 'I thought you were supposed to do whatever needs doing.'

He tosses his head. 'Yes, that's right. Sometimes it's counselling.'

'Well, we don't actually *need* a counsellor at the moment,' I say sarcastically. 'It's light housework that wants doing.'

I stride upstairs and go in to see John. He has never met Maurice because he has always been in bed when he comes, but is irritated by everything he has heard about him. We talk while Maurice goes into the bathroom, makes a few cleaning noises and then goes downstairs again. When I go to inspect what he has done, I cannot see any difference. The dust is still there on the top of the marble shelf.

My rage is building up. Downstairs, I find Maurice flicking a duster around the room with angry jerks of the hand.

'Is there anything else you would like me to do?' he asks with a sneer.

I look at the dirty carpet on the stairs. 'You could Hoover the stairs.' I say it as simply as I can, but I know it sounds provocative.

Sure enough, Maurice takes a deep breath and snorts. 'I'm here to help John, not clean up after his friends.'

I feel something snap inside me.

'Get out!' At first my voice is low, but then it rises as my rage overwhelms me. 'Get out of here right now!'

Maurice looks a bit shaken, but he stands his ground. 'I'm here to work, to look after John.'

'Get out!' I repeat as I stamp to the front door and open it. 'Right now. I'll be making a complaint about you to the Council.'

I am quite shocked by my sudden imperious manner. Is this me, or is it my grandmother talking to her servants?

Maurice picks up his jacket and creeps out. 'Stupid bitch!' He mutters it loudly enough for me to hear.

I run upstairs to find John grinning at me. 'Well done!' he says. 'Did you throw him out? I've been dying to get rid of him for ages, but the Council kept sending him.'

I think John is finally pleased to have 'bossy Emma' do the dirty work for him. When we were children, he and Adam were constantly complaining about my bossiness. There is no complaint today!

For the next hour I try to contact the relevant man at the Council to tell him about Maurice's behaviour. When he finally returns my call, I can tell that Maurice has already got there first with his version of the story.

But I am not interested in winning any arguments. My message is clear. The Council should not be sending people like Maurice into the homes of dying men and women where there are already enough edgy and competitive individuals on the scene. And Maurice is not to come again. I tell him he can talk to Jacques to confirm all this.

After this, Maurice no longer comes to Alwyne Road.

Instead, two very quiet and pleasant helpers come and do what they are supposed to do, and then leave. Later we hear from them that Maurice has been sacked, so I feel vindicated.

Apart from packing, I have one more thing to do before we set off on holiday. I must organise John's funeral, in case he dies while we are away. This way, everyone will be briefed about what to do.

I telephone Colin Lewis, an undertaker in Chichester who was at the Midhurst Grammar School with my Uncle Edwin. Colin, I hate to say, is the family undertaker. He buried my grandfather in 1968; Edwin's wife, my aunt, in 1982 and my brother Simon in 1989. No doubt he will bury Oma when she finally dies. I am in a hurry and I would like to deal with someone who is not a total stranger.

When I telephone, Colin is out but his wife, who works with him, answers. I explain the situation and say that we are booked to go on holiday so we need to get the details sorted out in advance.

Mrs Lewis is wonderfully understanding and does not make me feel hard-hearted for wanting to go away. She tells me Colin will ring back, which he does within the hour.

Colin is immediately helpful; he grasps the situation and explains exactly what will happen if John dies while Dick and I are in France. I write everything down. Since John is in London and Colin in Chichester, and the funeral will be in London, Colin feels that there is no point in collecting his body and taking it back to Chichester. He says he can arrange for a contact at the Co-op undertakers to look after the body until the funeral.

I give him our French telephone numbers, and also Jacques' numbers, all just in case. I feel detached and organised; I talk without any emotion in my voice. It is weird to sound so cold and unfeeling, but I know it is necessary to keep my imagination out of it for the time being.

It all sounds very straightforward and practical, and I am happy to have the arrangements sorted out. I don't ask about the price, but Colin sounds me out about the kind of wood we want for the coffin. I assume that when I say it should be the basic model, he understands that we are not planning a fancy funeral but a simple cremation and a secular ceremony which Dick and I have yet to plan. I ask him to send the bill to my mother. It seems harsh for her to pay for her son's funeral, but I don't know what else to do. The expenses for Simon's funeral were met out of his estate. The problem now, as everyone except Jacques realises, is that there will be no estate for John.

I telephone Adam to tell him what the plans are while we are away. He is sounding pretty exasperated. A lot of telephone discussions have been going on between him and John about Jacques and money.

John is still pestering Adam about looking after Jacques financially once he dies. Adam has emphasised that the £40,000 pension fund pay-out that is definitely due on John's death must be used to pay off debts. As a trustee, he has refused John's request to pay it over to Jacques.

Now John is trying another tack. He has the wild idea that Adam should pay Jacques a basic salary matching Adam's for a period of three years following his death. Adam is incensed by this suggestion. 'I've told John that it would be a disincentive if every time I wrote myself a cheque from the business, I had to write one for Jacques, too. I wrote telling John I am furious about the enormous credit card bills he's been running up and his complete disregard for the mess he is leaving behind.'

Adam says he broke the 'three-day rule' for angry letters

and sent it straight away. John has just rung him to say he is distraught that the two people he loves most in the world are at each other's throats. 'Now he's trying to renegotiate the payment period to eighteen months.'

Finally, Adam says, he agreed to pay the mortgage on Alwyne Road for three months after John's death so that Jacques can have time to find alternative accommodation.

I can tell from his tone of voice that this is a major concession on Adam's part, and I agree. Jacques' expectations are hard to understand and it infuriates me that John feeds them in this way.

I have had enough of all this. Thank God we're going on holiday.

With the funeral all sorted out, I pack our bags. I long to get off to France away from all the illness and the squabbling.

Chapter Nine

France, 30 July – 13 August

We have rented a *gite* in the Perche region of Normandy, which is very beautiful – not unlike Sussex, with dense broadleaf woods and rich agricultural land. Blotchy grey and white Normandy cattle and solid Percheron horses dot the luscious green fields around.

The house is quite a way outside the village and set apart in a large garden abutting farm buildings and fields beyond. In the nearest field there is a pond surrounded by bulrushes and tall reeds, the favourite haunt of a large blue heron which frequently stands in the water on one leg, patiently waiting to scoop up a fish or a frog with its long beak.

We have struck lucky with the accommodation, too. The comfortable old farmhouse is clearly the regular weekend retreat of the Parisian owners. It has a well equipped kitchen and comfortable furniture. Being American, Dick does not believe in the spartan approach to holidays and dreads badly equipped self-catering kitchens. He travels with his own cook's essentials: his sharp kitchen knives and steel wrapped up in a thick canvas holder, and if possible a chopping board.

Souvenirs from all over the world are dotted around – obviously the owners are great travellers – and books are everywhere. I try to work out who they are and what they do. I can tell that they have one child, a daughter, that the wife is British and the husband French. They are clearly well-heeled, though with no obvious passions or interests. We speculate about their occupations, and in view of their extensive world travels we decide they are either diplomats or spies.

It is wonderfully quiet. The road is small and rarely used except by the occasional tractor, and the children have plenty of room to run around. They play baseball with Dick in the garden. I have brought my water-colours and we paint pictures of each other and of the garden.

We explore the nearby towns and villages. There is La Ferte-Vidame, with the ruins of a château belonging to the family of Duc de Saint-Simon, the French courtier and author, where he retired in 1723 to write most of his *Memoires*. I have not, of course, ever read these *Memoires*, but I know about them because a grateful patient once gave them to Peter – two massive doorstops of volumes, which sat for years in my mother's consulting room in Devonshire Place.

On our first day we walk around the park beside the ruins, as the children run ahead and throw stones into the ponds. Later we eat excellent traditional French food in the restaurant down the road.

In the restaurant, the children start discussing John. I think they must have been talking to each other about him, for suddenly – after weeks showing almost a lack of interest – all kinds of fantasies have been unleashed. They talk endlessly about death and what happens when you die. They have already seen one uncle dead; how can another one be dying so soon? How can John die before their great-grandmother, Oma, who is so much older?

They quiz us with questions to which we have few answers. At times I wish I had a belief that enabled me to give out simple answers, a check list that I could look up at will. But there are no stock replies and I end up feeling weepy or angry, afraid of what the next few weeks are to bring. We go on living, as we have to, but the crisis is rapidly accelerating towards us.

In France, however, we can ignore it for a while. We shop at the markets and persuade the children to come into churches long enough for Dick and me to see the interiors. Then we discover Soligny la Trappe, a lake in the middle of the Forêt du Perche, with water-slides and other delights for the girls. We take picnics for lunch, which we eat in the woods before spending the hot afternoons in the water.

We read and sleep a lot, and eat and drink a lot too. Dick cooks a delicious meal nearly every night. Ruth needs a good nap in the afternoons still, and I find that I am cat-napping at the same time, often lying on the sofa with her sprawled out across my belly. I never used to be able to sleep in the day. Perhaps I'm getting old, but I suspect I have simply found a way of shutting out most of my waking thoughts.

Of course, we don't blot out Alwyne Road completely. We have bought a phone card and every other day we keep on the look-out for phone boxes that will take cards so that I can telephone John. Suddenly, I switch from being a relaxed person on a holiday schedule to an anxious big sister ready to hear the worst. Every time I ring, I can feel my heart racing as I wait for the phone to be answered, anticipating a change in the circumstances, suddenly being told that John has deteriorated or died.

But it is not to be. Each time, it looks as though we shall see out the entire fortnight in France. John's condition seems relatively stable. Sometimes he is awake and happy to talk, at other times he is sleeping and I speak to Jacques, Paul or Robbie.

One Sunday morning when I speak to John, he sounds bizarrely cheerful. It is early, but in France the sky is a deep blue and the sun already hot. John says it's a beautiful day in London, too: that he is feeling 'top of the morning'. His voice is strong. I am pretty sure that he will last until we get back.

When I put the telephone down I think how weird it is that someone can be close to death and say that they feel 'top of the morning'. But John has always been able to separate the feelings he expresses from those he feels. When he was about eleven and went on a ski-ing holiday organised by Erna Low, he sent back a postcard saying, 'Dear Mummy, I am having a lovely time. I hate the leader and the leader hates me. Love, John.'

That Sunday is a memorable day. We have an exquisite meal in Verneuil-sur-Avre where all the children behave and find enough food they can eat happily. It seems like a watershed. Now at last our children are sufficiently civilised to eat in proper restaurants! Even the French customers notice and, to my pride, are nodding with approval at *les petites Anglaises*.

A few days later I call again, this time from the telephone booth in the square in Longny. It is late afternoon and unbearably hot. Sweat drips down my back as I speak to Robbie, who tells me he is sitting beside the sleeping John.

'He's very weak now,' Robbie says, 'and he's lost a lot of weight.'

The seriousness in Robbie's voice tells me that the situation is shifting slightly. This does seem like a change, but I cannot imagine that John can lose even more weight than he has already.

The holiday has been so successful and restful that I have been lulled into feeling that this state of affairs will go on for ever. But as we head back to Caen to catch the ferry home, I feel myself getting tense again, braced for what the next few weeks will bring.

Chapter Ten

13 August

We return to London to find that most of the building work at the house has been finished, but not *quite* all. New paving stones which have been laid outside the kitchen door are the wrong kind, not what I requested, but I don't have the energy to object. I am disappointed that after all these weeks the extension is still not completed, the builders are not yet out of our lives; but I am mainly pleased to see that the new room – my new study – has been growing and developing while we have been in France.

There is a note from Anne. Thinking that the builders had finished, she cleaned the house for us while we were away. Then they returned without warning and messed it up again. All her hard work was a waste of time for her and a waste of money for us. Dave, she informs us, wants the balance of his money, though there are still bits and pieces to be finished off – and my mother's table has not yet appeared, either.

I am annoyed about the builders but more anxious to see John. Leaving Dick and the children at home, I drive over by myself on Sunday evening.

Downstairs, the house seems busy. Jacques and David are there; Paul and Robbie are in and out; Imogen comes over for the evening.

John is upstairs. I go up and stand in the bedroom doorway and watch him as he dozes in his bed. I am shocked to see how much thinner he has become since I last saw him just over two weeks ago – Robbie was right. He now looks truly cadaverous; his face is that of a skeleton, sunk so much that his eyelids are only half closed even though he is asleep. The hair on his head is dull and thin. His body is now completely emaciated so that his skin and remaining flesh hang from his long bones. His skull is clearly defined, with huge sunken eyes and receding lips. His ribs are sticking out and he lies so still and unmoving that only the pulsating throb of his heart beating under the taut skin of his ribcage indicates that he is still alive. Perhaps the most shocking sight of all is the purple blotches of Kaposi's sarcoma spreading over his legs and arms. So now I know what it looks like . . .

When I call out his name softly, he wakes slowly and shifts in the bed. He has special clear plasters on his elbows where angry bed sores have appeared. He has another, larger one around his buttocks where the diarrhoea has made his skin raw. Pads like opened nappies have been placed strategically under him to prevent him soiling the bed. I am glad that he is not actually wearing them, like the baby he used to be.

John looks up and says hello. But his voice has none of the enthusiasm of recognition; it sounds weary and comes out as a raspy whisper. I see a sad, pleading look in his eyes, as if he is apologising for his appearance. His lips are dry, encrusted with some kind of mucus that sits in his mouth. I guess this must be the oral thrush that many HIV people suffer from. There are some little yellow sponges on sticks beside his bed. I dip one in water and wipe it across his parched lips.

It is warm in the house and there are only white sheets on the bed. The top sheet is twisted around his left leg, which looks like the limb of a skeleton but with skin on.

John now resembles those patients I used to observe in the AIDS ward. He has the sad staring eyes, the collapsed but tight cheeks, the pallid skin and a head that looks too heavy for his thin neck to support. I used to wonder how long it would take for John to look like that. Now I know – it has been eight months. It must be close to the end.

John asks about our French holiday in a polite sort of way, but when I begin to describe the house and the countryside, I feel I am exhausting him. I can tell he is hardly listening. I am also aware how I sound; as if to make up for the weakness of his voice, I seem to have adopted a pseudo-cheerful tone and manner. I must stop doing this.

John's eyelids droop as he drops off to sleep again in front of me. There is no sound except for the hum of the fridge in the corner and the whirr of the driver as it pumps another dose of diamorphine into his veins at regular intervals.

However weak he looks, John's condition is still fairly stable. The routine at Alwyne Road is well established. I arrange to be there later in the week, but decide not to visit the next day. It is a relief not to feel that I must rush up there from work on my first day back.

Back at the office, Linda and Nadia, *She*'s art director, are now away on holiday in Cyprus with their families so I am officially in charge of the magazine, which makes me nervous. If anything does go wrong, I shan't be in a fit state to sort it out.

I am lucky that Jan is there and relieved again to have her around, ready to help out and back me up when necessary. As yet there are no obvious problems with the issue, and no major decisions need to be made.

I telephone Colin the undertaker to let him know that I am now back from holiday and that John is still alive. Rebecca and Alice, the two older girls, have gone off to New York – travelling as unaccompanied minors – to stay with Dick's parents for the rest of their summer holidays. Ruth remains at home with Dick and me. Our house seems odd and empty without two of our girls.

On Tuesday, everything changes. It is like having a new-born baby; just when you think a routine has been established, you are proved wrong. When I call the house from work, Jacques says that the palliative care doctors think John now has bacterial pneumonia and are debating whether to give him antibiotics.

John himself is confused about what he wants. On the one hand, he says he does not want his life prolonged unnecessarily; on the other, he is terrified of suffocating. The idea of not being able to catch his breath, of not having air in his lungs, has frightened him for some time. When I get up to the house that evening, I am therefore unsurprised to learn that John has decided that he will take the antibiotics after all.

Since we returned from France, it seems that the tension in the house has grown. The differences are coming out, the questions about who is in charge are being raised again.

For instance, there is much talk about increasing the diamorphine to make John calmer. Jacques is still opposed to this idea, as he clearly worries that John will be too knocked out to communicate with him any more. The opposing view is that since John can hardly say anything now, it seems cruel to keep him so close to consciousness. The look of fear in his staring eyes tells us that.

Everyone is anxious to be sensitive to Jacques' wishes, yet there is a growing feeling that he is being selfish. It is not as if he and John are together any more, anyway. They have not been a couple for years. Jacques has David, solid, dependable David, always there in the background as a support.

As the days go by, John grows weaker and the tensions build. I can sense that Paul and Jacques are at odds with one another. Adam is in New York, still caught up in the ongoing lawsuit against the old employee who set up a new company and stole a lot of their clients (a typical battle for them). He cannot leave before that is over. Jacques is getting more and more exhausted from constantly broken nights sleeping in John's room, and it is now necessary to arrange for proper nursing care at night. Imogen sets to work sorting this out, and it is arranged that Macmillan nurses will come for the late-night shift.

The first night when one of these nurses comes, she is astonished to find John downstairs, more or less mobile, sipping a glass of champagne. Earlier that day, Adam had rung from New York to say that they have won their case. The rejoicing was considerable and the news injected some extraordinary energy into John, who asked to be carried downstairs for the celebratory barbecue in the garden.

That is the last time he ever sets foot downstairs.

On Friday, 19 August, Adam arrives from New York and comes up to the house accompanied by Kenny Everett in whose flat he is staying while he is over here. He is planning to stay for two weeks. No one says anything, but it is clear that we hope it will all be over within that time.

I am interested to meet Kenny, who Adam has assured me is a great guy. I had once admired him as a disc jockey, but I was put off by his famous 'Bomb the Russians!' outburst and his support for Mrs Thatcher. However, Adam says Kenny is not in the slightest bit interested in politics and remains deeply embarrassed about his silly comments, which he has never been allowed to forget.

Kenny comes to the house, flamboyant and making jokes. He is an incredibly funny person. While Adam goes upstairs to see his brother, Kenny stays downstairs and has some tea with us. He is polite to Dick and me and seems relaxed about the prospect of seeing John, whom he last saw a couple of months ago. I know from Adam and from the newspapers that Kenny is HIV-positive, too. He was captured on film by one of the paparazzi as he was leaving St Stephen's Hospital one day, after an attack of PCP.

Mindful of how shocked I was to see John after a gap of only two weeks, I want to warn Kenny. 'He's very thin,' I say. 'He's lost a lot of weight.' I notice a blotch of purple skin on Kenny's neck; I know what that is.

Kenny laughs and tosses his head. 'Oh, I saw him quite recently,' he says blithely. 'He was already thin then.'

I want to repeat my warning, but there is no point. Kenny will see soon enough.

When Adam comes downstairs, it is Kenny's turn to go up. Ten minutes later he comes down again, looking subdued and visibly shocked. I watch him across the room. It must be so frightening to see people ahead of you going down the path towards certain death, revealing what awaits you too. Poor Kenny. Apart from that violaceous patch on his neck, he looks perfectly fit. Yet within eight months he too will be dead.

Kenny is a warm man. I can tell that he likes Dick and me. He gives me a kiss and a hug.

Dick likes him too. 'You must come to dinner while Adam is over,' he volunteers. Dick is not a very sociable person, but he loves to cook for people he takes to.

'Oooh, I'd love a home-cooked meal,' says Kenny, wonderfully camp. 'I hardly ever get one of those.'

Back home, the builders are putting the finishing touches to our extension at last. Downstairs, in our enlarged laundry room, the shower has been built, the lavatory reinstalled and the washing machine and drier repositioned and plumbed in. Upstairs, the landing loo has been pushed sideways into a tiny but functional room, leaving a small landing which leads into my study, looking down across our small London garden. I can now move in my mother's Victorian desk from Devonshire Place, which has been sitting in my old study while the building work continued. Originally it came from my great-grandparents' house in Bletchingly before moving to the Dulwich house. The drawers rattle with small objects from the past – an ancient Parker fountain pen, now clogged with dry ink, some labels left over from the move to Devonshire Place from Dulwich; the odd unidentifiable pill from my parents' medical practice. It has the comforting, familiar appearance of a reliable member of the family. There is something solid about it that I have always known. I can still picture one or other of my parents sitting at it, writing articles or books in longhand.

I love the fact that this desk goes back for generations. It is not a grand piece of furniture; my mother thinks it was probably originally the butler's desk, or the housekeeper's. I like that, too.

The desk makes me think about the people who have sat at it in the past, and those who have lived before me. I have always been fascinated by family history. When I was a child and staying at my grandparents' house, I would escape from tedious adult conversation by poring over the photograph albums in the corner of the drawing room. This was considered an acceptable way to withdraw from grown-up company, yet I was able to maintain communication because I would pester my grandmother to identify the characters in the pictures.

It has always been the men in the family who have taken the photographs. First my great-grandfather, who recorded his family's grand life in their country mansion on a hill in Surrey, with his large extended family of Russian, German and American cousins. The grandeur of their style of living was also captured by his nephew, my grandmother's cousin, the great photographer Bill Brandt. These pictures were taken from a very different perspective – the white-capped maid drawing water for her mistress's bath, my great-grandparents playing bridge in Mayfair, a cocktail party at Bletchingly one warm summer afternoon – all during the 1930s, when millions were starving.

Later it was my grandfather, a controversial stipendiary magistrate in his day, who was the keen photographer. He recorded the lives of my mother and aunt and uncle, this time during the War in their home in Epsom. In my mind's eye I retain the contents of whole albums – two little girls in hand-knitted shorts and Milly Molly Mandy haircuts, 'fishing' off a wall in their sunny garden. My grandmother, dark-haired and glamorous, taking her two small daughters to school in the pony-trap. A photo of two little girls reading the letter which brings the news that their baby brother Edwin has been born.

For a brief time before he got polio, it was my father who took the family photographs, even developing the film. When I was a child, photographic equipment lay abandoned on the work benches in the dark cellar in Dulwich, near the cupboard that housed a box with human bones wrapped in newspaper – pieces of Peter's father's skeleton from medical school.

Among my siblings, it was John who developed a passion for photography which lasted for some years. He produced hundreds of prints of his family and friends. In fact, the only photographs of any of us as teenagers and young adults were taken and developed by Johnny in the dark-room at his school, where he and his friends had hidden the entire contents of the tuckshop.

Everything I think about at the moment seems to come back to John.

Dave, the builder, now wants the balance of his money. We have paid him most of what we owe him, but I am reluctant to hand over the final payment of £1,000 until he has finished off the very last details. Also, there is the matter of the table which he took away for his 'mate' to renovate. This has still not reappeared after three months, and I want to get it back before Dave himself disappears.

On the Friday, 19 August, Dave calls to ask for his money. It is early morning and an awkward moment as I am about to leave home to get to a meeting at work and then go on up to John's house. I cannot see myself getting to the bank and back home to pay Dave until the following week; he will just have to be patient.

'I'm very sorry,' I say dramatically, 'but my brother is on his death-bed and you'll have to wait until next week for payment.' This is only partly the reason, though. I simply do not want to give him his money until everything has been finished off satisfactorily.

'Sorry about your brother. I'll come for it on Monday, then,' says Dave.

Afterwards, I realise that I forgot to mention the table.

With only Ruth at home, the house is very quiet in the evenings. After work I concentrate on my novel, which has to be finished in September. It has recently been going remarkably well.

When Ruth is in bed, Dick cooks supper and I potter around the garden, pulling up weeds and cutting back overgrown blooms. The night air is warm and close, almost sweaty and feverish. Sitting on the wooden bench out in my garden, I breathe in the sweet smell of the jasmine and enjoy the sight of the heavy blooms of the pale pink mallow which was just a small cutting from Wiblings late last year when Philip gave it to me.

I think of John's decaying body withering away in his stuffy bedroom. The mallow has thrived and bloomed during the very period when he has been declining. It will probably live for a couple of years yet – not for very long, but John must be just days away from the end of his life.

The next day, Sunday, 20 August, we go to visit John. It is Mark's birthday but he and his family are away in France; as is Jane.

My mother and Philip are at the house, having driven up from Sussex as usual. Adam, Imogen, David and Paul are also there. The palliative care team have been and gone. It was Imogen's birthday the day before and they had held a little party. John had asked Jacques to buy Imogen a present for him.

Jacques bought her a pretty little chest of drawers from a shop in Islington selling Indian products. I admire it and want one for myself, as it is the perfect size for my jewellery. As Jacques and I drive down to Islington to buy food supplies at Marks & Spencer, I feel self-conscious as if we are in a film. Little details continue even when there is another major drama being played out.

In Marks & Spencer, we walk up and down the aisles and I am surprised by what Jacques is buying – chops and vegetables, humus, bread and crackers. At first I think he's catering for everyone in the house, but then I realise that he has only John in mind. 'Oh, John likes this kind,' he says, reaching for the taramasalata.

I don't think John can eat such foods any more. He does not look strong enough to suck through a straw, let alone chew and swallow proper food.

'Are you sure you need all this?' I ask.

Jacques does not respond, and I don't push it.

Afterwards, Jacques takes me to the Indian shop where I buy a small chest of drawers for myself. It is £40, not cheap but I feel extravagant.

During our shopping trip, Jacques and I talk. In spite of the problems about John's money, I am fond of him and feel a closeness that goes back several years now. Through our work, we have quite a number of acquaintances in common, and we gossip about those and others.

Then I discover the thinking behind Jacques' food purchases as he talks about what he means to cook for supper. He says he believes that if John eats then he will get stronger and build up his immune system so that he will be better able to fight off the opportunistic infections that attack AIDS patients. I don't have the heart to contradict him, and I listen in wonder. Jacques' words seem crazy in the circumstances. Surely he can see that it is a bit late for building up John's body? Surely my poor brother should be allowed to waste away quietly? It seems almost cruel to consider feeding him up just so that he can linger for a few more weeks. Still, I say nothing. I don't want to hurt Jacques' feelings by pointing out what seems obvious to me.

When we get home, everyone is upstairs around John's bed. My mother sits close to his head. Every now and then, she wets his parched lips with one of the little yellow swabs dipped in water.

We all talk politely to each other, but I sense the now familiar tension between Jacques and Adam and Paul.

Ruth stumbles excitedly around John's bedroom. She finds it extraordinary that a grown-up is in bed in the middle of the afternoon. When John inclines his head towards her and smiles, the creases around his mouth are like sharply folded paper. Then she marches up and down, in and out of the bedroom, into the bathroom and around the landing, chanting away in her singsong voice, 'John die! John die!'

Adam, Dick and I catch each other's eyes. Dick coaxes Ruth into a corner and offers her a sweet to distract her. She is enjoying herself, regarding herself the centre of attention among all these adults. No one else seems to have heard her little chant, though it would hardly have mattered if they had. And John certainly does not seem to have heard. If he had, I think he would have smiled still.

John's lips are so parched, and still covered with the dry mucus discharge from the oral thrush. A plate of red watermelon is lying by his bed, placed there by Paul who went down to the shops to buy it at John's request. When John sucks a slice, his hand is unsteady and he drips pink juice down his face and bare chest. Imogen wipes it off with a professional firmness.

Ruth is restless, so my mother and I take her out for some fresh air. We go over the road to the New River Walk, a pretty public garden that follows the route of the early seventeenth-century aqueduct. Ruth chases the ducks and runs ahead of us laughing. If we speak at all, we talk about Ruth, so full of life. But there is not much to say about anything.

At least it is a beautiful day. Heavy weeping willows drape over the water. Ducks hide in the reeds. The garden is busy with Londoners out for a walk with their families on this hot Saturday afternoon. I wonder idly how many of them have a close relative on his death-bed at that very moment. Mum was present when Ruth was born; two years later she is watching her son die.

The next day, Sunday, we go over again at midday. The boys are all there. We sit on cushions on the roof of the kitchen and read the Sunday papers. There is an oddly cosy Sunday afternoon atmosphere. It has a timeless quality, as if this has been going on for ever, and will continue for ever after. This afternoon the tension has subsided. There is almost a softness in the air, a closeness, the camaraderie among the regular visitors to the house who are drawn together by this common purpose – to see John out. But it is clear that in spite of the closeness, we long to be done with the routine. We feel defeated by the certainty of the outcome, and by the agony of each individual moment in which the end seems both imminent and remote. No one says this, but we all feel it.

The next day is Monday. Linda and Nadia are still away and I remain officially in charge. Still nothing bad has happened.

When I go to John's after work, he is looking very frightened. But now he is so thin that his face has a permanently startled look. Smiles are grimaces, grimaces smiles. His voice is a croaky whisper. As he watches me bustling around to do things for him, he asks with a soft sigh, 'How do you have so much energy?'

That evening at about 7.30, Imogen comes over after work. She has just attended a home birth down the road. 'A home birth and a home death – a nice balance,' she says quietly. As a doctor, her perspective must be so different from ours. She talks to my parents, both doctors, in a language that differs from ours too.

The palliative care team has decided it is best to stop the antibiotics and allow the pneumonia to take its course. This is a major decision. There is talk about increasing the dose of diamorphine, but Jacques is still reluctant to agree to this, still afraid to lose contact with John. What difference does it really make at this stage? The friction builds; we whisper in clusters around the house. It appears that Jacques is the only one who wants to cling on to John. To the rest of us it seems so cruel. Who should have the say here? Imogen says she will talk to Jacques; her diplomacy is impressive.

When Dick and I get home from Alwyne Road, it seems that Dave has been to the house and finished all the building work at last. Anne says he seemed annoyed that I have not left him his money. Tough, I think. He may have finished the work, but I still want the table back. That table is my mother's; it does not even belong to me.

The next day, Tuesday, 23 August, I go over to John's house to spend the whole morning there. I take some work, some articles to edit. Most of the time John is asleep upstairs. I come up to check on him every fifteen minutes. Occasionally he is awake and looks at me. I am aware that it is important not to try to be too sunny. I must allow him to be sad, and let him see that I am sad. I hold his hand gently and he drifts back to sleep.

I go downstairs and try to work again. This is like having a baby but worse. A tiny incontinent creature that will grow to be an independent being is very different from an incontinent adult man facing death on his own. I dread John wanting to go to pee in the bathroom, as I do not think I will be able to support him across the room. But at some point he wants to, and I have to. As his six-feet-three-inch frame wraps itself around my shoulders, I feel very short. Fortunately, Robbie appears as I am struggling to get him next door; he grabs John before he crumples on the floor.

Remarkably, John is still slightly sun-tanned – mainly from sitting outside in the sun for a few weeks in July and early August, I expect.

Late morning and Paul arrives, cheerful as always. He is the ever-loyal friend and has arrived with his regular large watermelon which he cuts up to present to John in a bowl.

Jacques also comes home, having managed to put in some hours at his workshop. He too has some food supplies and is angry when he sees Paul's watermelon. 'You'll ruin his appetite!' he shouts.

Things have come to a head. Clearly incensed by Jacques' remark, Paul jumps to his feet. 'John should be allowed to eat what he likes. He wanted watermelon, so I got it for him.'

Jacques glares at him. 'You'll ruin his appetite,' he repeats. 'No wonder he doesn't eat properly.'

It seems a stupid argument anyway, since John is not eating anything at all, not even the watermelon, but I am on Paul's side. There is no point in fighting the inevitable.

But Jacques and Paul are angry. They square up and one of them lashes out at the other. Before they both launch themselves into a fist-fight, Robbie grabs them and pushes them apart. 'Boys, boys,' he says in a calm and authoritative voice. I am impressed. Robbie is easily the youngest of the three but seems more mature generally. I am also relieved, for I certainly would not have been able to intervene; they are not my brothers.

That day Dick has spoken to Dave and asked about the table. Dave tells him he returned it weeks ago, claiming that he brought it back early one morning and left it outside the house.

I do not believe this story but, even if it were true, an antique table left outside a house at any time of day would disappear in a flash in our neighbourhood. And Dave knows it.

When Dick reports the conversation, I am both furious and confused. I am afraid to tell my mother. I know it's only a table, but it came from her grandparents' house and has sentimental value. I think it will seem like just another painful loss at this point. That evening we turn on the answerphone. I cannot cope with the thought of dealing with Dave if he rings.

The following day is Wednesday, and it is very busy at work. We are beginning to think about planning the magazine's December schedule, as we always do at this time of year. It seems depressing planning the Christmas issue in the height of summer – but then we plan the summer issues in the depths of winter, which compensates. I also have to attend a big meeting about the *She* Family Cook competition we are organising with Granada TV, sponsored by Tesco. As Dick is the food editor of *She*, he is one of the judges, so we are both involved in it. (This competition would subsequently result in Granada TV being fined a record £500,000 by the ITC, the TV watchdog, for product placement.)

I am tired when I return home. It is hot and muggy. Ruth goes to bed without any trouble and Dick and I settle down for a quiet dinner. There is no significant news from Canonbury.

At about 8 o'clock the telephone rings. As I put the receiver to my ear and say 'Hello', I can hear a man's voice shouting, 'I hope you and your partner have a fucking good bone surgeon; you'll need one after what I'm going to do to you!'

He needs no introduction. It is Dave. I try to remain calm as the tirade continues: 'You lied to me. You told me your brother was dead and now I hear he's still alive.'

He sounds drunk, but even so I cannot believe he is complaining about this. 'I told you he's on his death-bed, and he still is.' I am astonished to find myself suddenly wondering if I had used the expression incorrectly. If someone is on their death-bed, does that mean they are dead or about to die any minute? I ought to know, but now I don't. This is ridiculous.

Dave hesitates. Does he really believe that I lied about my brother dying?

'Well, me and my kids need that money, do you hear?'

'Where's my table, Dave?'

'I told your husband, I left it outside your door at six o'clock one morning.'

'And you didn't tell us?' I am both upset and furious. Taking a deep breath, I go on the attack. 'You're going to have to wait a bit longer for your money until I've consulted a lawyer about this situation.' I know it is a provocative remark, but I am damned if I will be bullied.

Dave begins to bellow down the telephone again about all the things he is going to do, including break every bone in my body.

Dick grabs the telephone from me and switches it off. Then he turns on the tape recorder on the answering machine and rings Dave back, trying to get him to repeat his threats on the phone. He is partially successful.

We telephone the police, who come round within ten minutes to take a statement. They tell me that it is a civil matter and not for them, but reassure me that if Dave appears on the doorstep I should call them out again. I sense they are a little disappointed that he is not actually prowling around the neighbourhood.

Later Dick calls Dave back and tells him that his behaviour has been reported to the police. He informs him that his money – minus a couple of hundred for the lost table – will be ready for him in the morning, if he cares to collect it.

Dick and I spend what's left of the evening in shock. This is surreal. My brother is dying, and we are receiving death threats from a builder. However, I am still capable of laughing when I remember that in the early days of our acquaintance, I was recommending Dave the builder to our friends. And I know that in the future our 'builder story' will top anyone else's. But I feel it's a shame that I cannot tell my mother about it, because I think she will be upset about her table. Otherwise, I believe she would laugh. It is several years before I do tell her.

Chapter Eleven

25 August

Soon after 8 o'clock the next morning, Thursday, Imogen telephones to ask if I can come over to the house straight away. She needs to leave for her practice and Jacques is anxious to see that everything is going well at the shop. I am scheduled to spend the morning at Alwyne Road anyway, and was about to call a minicab to take me over there.

When I get to the house, Jacques has already gone and Imogen is ready to leave. She says that John had a bad night and has been panicking. 'He's lapsing in and out of consciousness now,' she explains. 'Most of the time he's not distressed but occasionally he is, so I've given him some extra sedation.'

Imogen also explains that John is now fitted with a kind of condom with a tube into which he can pee, so he doesn't have to worry about getting to the bathroom. Her energy astounds me. She seems to be able to function on so little sleep. As she

leaves for her surgery, she says she will drop in again at lunch-
time to see how John is.

After she has gone, I make myself a cup of coffee and drink
it downstairs. The house is wonderfully quiet. Tsar, the cat,
sedately paces the downstairs sitting room. On the floor by the
elegant tall French windows is Peter's collection of wooden
elephants, which he gave to John a few months ago when
Devonshire Place was sold.

I have known these elephants all my life, as they sat on the
mantelpiece in my father's study in Dulwich and then on the
bookshelves in his flat. We used to play with them when we
were children. Also on the mantelpiece was a wooden Buddha
and a black stone model of a bear – given to him by a patient, I
think. When I was about seven, I lovingly scratched 'Mummy'
along the bear's back – an unappreciated act that got me into
some trouble. The wobbly white letters are still there today.

These are objects from my past, my family past, and I am
sentimental about them. Also on the floor, leaning against the
wall, are prints from the house which my mother gave to John
when the Devonshire Place house was sold. I don't believe they
mean anything to John, who has never been particularly interested in art, but I think it was important that our parents gave
him pieces from the house, as they did to the rest of us, even
though he is dying.

I am sad to see a lovely marble Egyptian cat – also from
Peter, and also on the floor – now headless. Either a person or
the cat has knocked it over again. I feel annoyed that such
things are treated so casually here, but this time John can
hardly be to blame. And in any case, what do these objects
matter now? They mean nothing to John, who will probably
never see them. He will never come downstairs again in his
life.

When I go upstairs, John is sleeping soundly, breathing in deep, sighing breaths. His face is grey, his hair looks sparse and colourless rather than blond. The skin on his arms hangs from the bones more loosely even than before. His nose – broken by Paul in their first brawl at school, and once quite thick – is now thin and beaky. Seeing how deeply his eyes have sunk into his head, I am reminded of my grandfather, Opa, who died aged eighty.

John is thirty-five. From the strapping hulk he used to be, he has shrunk to a wizened old man. The tattoo on his upper arm, of a tiger leaping into the air, looked large, muscular and fierce just a few months ago. Now it too has shrunk, so that it looks starved and weak, no stronger than a pussy cat.

I have some work with me, but I cannot concentrate. I am fascinated by the sight of this dying boy. I wonder constantly about what is going on in his body at this precise moment which is different from what is happening in my own, healthy body. I imagine the armies of invaders gradually winning the battle now that the AIDS virus has paved the way for them, having destroyed John's immune system completely.

Looking at John in the bed, I wish again that I had a camera with me to take pictures of him, to capture this moment. I don't think he would mind . . . but perhaps he would. I am unsure how I would feel if I were in his place and someone was taking pictures of me that I would never see.

I also think they might be pictures I could not place in the family album for fear of shocking someone in the future. I would only be able to look at them furtively, like the piece of Simon's skull I have in a plastic bag in my cupboard. I have never shown that to anyone, except Dick, fearful that people will think it is a ghoulish thing to keep. I despise myself for caring.

Looking at John, I suddenly feel so exasperated, so sick of waiting and watching. It has been going on for too long now. I love my brother and do not want to lose him. I cannot bear to think about the loss of another sibling. But I also want him to be out of his misery. I want to be out of my own misery, too, if I am honest. There is no possibility that he can do anything other than deteriorate. The situation defies all optimism; my sense of impotence is almost unbearable.

I stare at John lying flat on his bed, his head twisted sideways. His mouth is open and a stream of saliva dribbles out of the corner to collect in a grey damp patch on the pillow. The whirr of the driver pumping the relieving heroin into his veins sounds like the roar of a train. I have a frightening urge to put a pillow over John's head and smother him, put him out of his misery, me out of mine, everyone else out of theirs.

This agonising temptation lasts for about a minute. Then, fortunately, my fantasy is interrupted by the ringing of the telephone. It is my sister Jane. I talk to her as I sit by John's bed; I tell her that I do not think it will be long now, but who knows? John seems to have the constitution of an ox. After I hang up, I realise that I have been speaking to Jane on the assumption that John cannot hear. I could be wrong: perhaps he can hear quite clearly. Perhaps he is just trapped inside his body, unable to communicate. I suddenly feel guilty about my insensitivity, but it is too late.

Suddenly, to my horror, John begins to surface. At first I think it is because he is upset or angry about what I said to Jane. He mumbles and moves his head, and frowns. I long for Imogen to be here. The sedative is wearing off and I am afraid of being on my own with him if he really starts to panic. I certainly won't know what to do. For a moment, I think I should telephone Imogen at her surgery.

John is struggling to get up but is too weak. Then I notice that he is trying to reach his crotch. 'It's all right,' I say quietly, as I would speak to one of my children, 'you won't wet the bed.'

I lift the sheet to see the contraption attached to his penis. John begins to get agitated and his struggling intensifies as he loses control of his bladder. Muttering a muffled apology, he sinks back into the pillow, relieved. He is unaware that the yellow urine is flowing down a tube and into a plastic bag on the floor, and not onto the bed. I am surprised how much urine there is, surprised that this collapsing body can still produce volumes of liquid waste. He has not eaten for days and can barely drink. It must be all that watermelon.

Seeing him like a little boy, as helpless as a baby, takes me back to the time when he was a baby and I, the experienced six-year-old, showed my baffled father how to put on his towelling nappy, safety-pin and all.

John was a huge, robust baby with a massive amount of physical energy. When he was about a year old, and crawling, we would put him at the bottom of the garden and watch him march along on hands and knees over the lawn, up the stone steps into the house, then up the six flights of stairs to the top floor. Then we would carry him down to the bottom of the garden to start all over again. John loved it. I can still see his grinning face as he crawled along with head up, elbows out, so proud of himself and delighted by the admiring response from all around him.

Around lunch-time, Adam and Jacques return. Then Imogen arrives, and is concerned to see that John is surfacing and agitated. She checks him over and when she tries to move him in the bed, he groans and winces – indicating, she explains, some level of distress.

After talking to Jacques for a while, she telephones one of the doctors on the palliative care team to discuss increasing the dose of diamorphine. This is a serious decision, and there is a formula for it. Usually the dose is doubled but this time, on the advice of the palliative care doctor, Imogen gives less than double. No more is necessary.

At last, John is going to have his wish and be put into a deeper sleep, so that he will not surface again. He will no longer be aware of his surroundings, no longer worry about anything, no longer be afraid. It also means that it is the last time he will hear us or be aware of any of us. This is goodbye.

Adam and I talk in a corner and agree that this should have been done much earlier. Now the decision has been taken, I feel angry that it was not reached before. It was cruel to keep John conscious for so long, to make him go through this long journey towards inevitable death, waiting for his body to pack up on its own. Why not give it a big push? Why not have it over and done with, as we would with a suffering animal? I wonder at the fact that I do not feel that there is something sacred about the very process of dying. Is there something wrong with those of us who want to hurry it along?

We all stand around the bed as Imogen prepares the diamorphine for this significant injection. Jacques gives John a dramatic kiss on the lips and holds his hand proprietorially. He looks devastated and I feel sorry for him, but I am also angry with him. We have all respected Jacques' feelings, but it has not necessarily been the best thing for my brother.

Imogen steps back from the bed.

'How long will it take?' I ask.

She puts her finger up to her mouth. 'Shh,' she says, moving to the landing. 'I'm never sure how much they can still hear, so it's best to assume they can.'

Her comment makes me even more regretful about having talked to Jane as I sat by his bed earlier.

'How long?' Adam asks now.

Imogen shrugs. 'I really don't know. One man took five days to die.'

I roll my eyes. 'Knowing John, it will take ages.' I feel desperate at the thought of more of these agonising days.

An hour later Dick arrives, then Paul and David after work. The usual group is settling in for the evening. I suddenly want to escape, I don't want to be there any more. Perhaps now that there is no more contact with John, I feel I can go . . . I can leave him.

I suddenly want to go out somewhere and, although Dick is reluctant, he agrees to go to a Thai restaurant in Kentish Town. When I go upstairs for one final look at John for the day, he is breathing very heavily and noisily. He will never hear me speak to him again.

We go home and, after getting Ruth ready for bed, I telephone my mother in Sussex and report on the latest from Alwyne Road. She has already spoken to Imogen. I tell her we are going to the Thai restaurant. We arrange for Anne to baby-sit while we walk up the road and have our meal.

The restaurant is empty apart from us. As we eat the delicately flavoured food, we talk very little, but I feel relieved to be away from that house.

At about 9.30, we have just finished the meal when I am vaguely aware of the telephone ringing. The man who has been serving us comes over to our table. 'Dally?' he says. 'Telephone for you.'

I leap to my feet and stumble across the room. It is Adam and I know what he is going to say even before he speaks.

'John's died. He died at seven-thirty this evening. We didn't know where you were until Mum told us.'

I drop the receiver, hardly able to believe it has happened at last. John died two hours ago and we did not know. Dick quickly pays the bill and we rush out into Junction Road and the dark night. Tears are streaming down my cheeks as we hurry down to Tufnell Park, over Lady Margaret Road and down to Falkland Road. I can hear Dick sobbing behind me. Anne already knows the news because Adam has been calling there. She offers to stay for as long as we need so that we can go over to Alwyne Road.

We take our final minicab to John's house. Downstairs is a crowd of people: the usual faces, but also members of Jacques' family – his parents and his sister. They speak French to each other and look sad as they sit on the sofa together. I hug everyone there in an uncharacteristically melodramatic way. I feel out of place somehow. They have been here for hours, but Dick and I were busy eating a Thai meal all this time. Although I never felt that I wanted to be at John's side at the very moment of his death – as Jacques did, I think – I had expected to be around. I was shocked by the eventual suddenness of it. No one dies at the right time.

As it was, John died alone. Imogen was lying out in the garden while Jacques, David and Robbie were watching television. Adam and Paul had just gone out to the shops. Surrounded by people for weeks, yet John died on his own. Perhaps he needed to be alone in order to let go. With childish satisfaction I am pleased that no one was at his side at the moment of death. No one could feel superior to anyone else.

Apparently it was Robbie, on his way to the lavatory, who noticed that John had stopped breathing.

Dick and I are late-comers and, since everyone has already paid their respects to the dead John, we do not have to wait but can walk up the stairs together and enter the bedroom once more.

John is lying flat on the bed, his head on a pillow. *Rigor mortis* is already beginning to set in – a reminder that he died several hours ago. His eyes are staring and a cloudy blue. His face is a waxy yellow and his lips, pulled back in a tight grin-grimace, are a translucent blue. I lean over and kiss him on the cold cheek. It is eerie to look at him and I am transfixed by the deadness of his body. I have now seen two dead bodies in my life, and both of them my brothers.

Dick and I cry silently as we stand by the bed. Adam comes up quietly and stands beside us. 'I suppose the virus is dead, too,' he says.

I lift up the sheet. Someone has removed the condom and John's penis lies flaccid against his leg. John was always sure of his sexuality, and he had liked sex. Sex, which gave him so much pleasure, was responsible for his death.

His long delicate fingers are waxy and stiffening; his finger-nails are the same shade of blue as his lips. I sit and study him for several long minutes. I did not get a chance to look closely at Simon's dead body all those years ago; his exploded head was not a sight for anyone. Our ancestors were accustomed to seeing dead bodies of all ages – old people, young women in childbirth, babies and children. Death was commonplace. It was even entertainment, too, with public executions and people being hung, drawn and quartered. Death was familiar to every-one, both at home and in public. It was not the taboo it has become now that people die in hospital and the nurses draw the curtains when they wheel out the latest casualty down to the morgue to protect the sensibilities of others in the ward.

How different John looks now from his appearance earlier that day, even in the semi-comatose state when at times it seemed that he had stopped breathing. This strange thing called life has left him; his body is literally lifeless. It seems unbelievable that he will never move, that he has gone and will not return. This is the day we have all been waiting for with morbid dread, yet now it is over and it is literally incredible. Everything seems to have come to a halt. It is almost impossible to grasp that the relentless nightmare is, in a way, over. Now there is simply the sadness of John's absence, and a dramatic sense of everything having ended. The anxiety, the misery, the excitement – they are all truly finished.

Downstairs we sit and drink and discuss the events of the day, endlessly going over the details of the exact time when everything happened. Robbie describes again how he went upstairs and realised that John had stopped his awful laboured breathing while everyone else was downstairs drinking tea. Our conversation is broken by quiet outbursts of sobbing. We reminisce, we cry and laugh and cry again. This is the day, John's death day.

The telephone rings and various people talk – Jacques, Adam, Paul. Even though the big windows are open and a balmy breeze comes in through the back door, the air in the room seems hot and clammy.

Tsar paces the room and winds his soft grey body around people's legs. Someone has replaced the head of the marble Egyptian cat, but not glued it. When Tsar brushes against it, the head falls again and rolls across the carpet.

At midnight, Dick and I leave. There is nothing more to say or do now. Tomorrow, much has to be done. I agree to come over in the morning, after I have spoken to Colin the undertaker about the funeral arrangements. We do not know when it will be. John has died just before the August bank holiday weekend, so nothing can be finalised until the following Tuesday. Jane and Matthew are on holiday in France, as are Mark and Clare and their children. They all need time to get back to London, too.

Chapter Twelve

26 August

The next morning I wake early and, full of energy, spring out of bed. I then drink several cups of black coffee, which makes me even more anxious as I wait for office hours to start.

The first call I make is to Colin, who is in his office by nine. He offers his condolences and runs through the plans again. He explains that he will arrange for John's body to be collected by the Co-op staff from Tottenham, who will keep it in their Chapel of Rest in Tottenham High Road. The details are so mundane that they could have come straight out of 'Monty Python'. After making enquiries, he tells me that the undertaker will be at Alwyne Road at around 11.30. He gives me the name of his contact at the Co-op but explains that since a bank holiday weekend is coming up, she may not be available all the time. This does not matter to me or anyone else in the family, since no one has expressed a wish to view John's body, and I tell Colin so. I feel confident that Colin has everything in hand. He will let us know when we can have the cremation, but he says the days after holiday weekends are always a busy time for crematoria.

After I have sorted out matters in London, I am planning to drive down to Sussex with Ruth after lunch for the weekend. I arrange to meet Colin later that afternoon, at Wiblings.

Next I telephone John's house and speak to David. He says that Jacques has spent the night in the same room as John, but that he is bearing up. I having a fleeting vision of Jacques sleeping by John's body, and think again how tolerant David is. I tell him that the undertakers are coming at 11.30.

David asks if they should dress John, as he is completely naked under the white sheet.

'Oh, I don't think so,' I say, unsure of what is expected. He's dead, so what's the point in dressing him up now?

Next, I telephone Jan at the office and tell her that John has died. As I say the words they come out as a sob, which annoys me. I had thought I was in control.

Jan assures me that everything is running smoothly and that I should not worry about the magazine. I tell her that I shall probably be off work for a week, by which time Linda and Nadia will be back from holiday anyway. Fortunately it is a relatively quiet time, with many people away on holiday and the main planning and scheduling all done in advance. I cannot imagine what I would have done if this were not the case. I would certainly be in a panic.

Now that the building work is over, we are having the outside paintwork done. The firm we are using is extremely professional and unobtrusive. After our experience with Dave, the quiet, well-mannered men are a relief. I am confident that there will be no death threats from them. One of them is like a little leprechaun – short and wizened, with a shock of thick white hair. I have noticed that he arrives early and waits to see movement in the kitchen before ringing the doorbell to start. Still, however well trained they are, it is unsettling to have four or five men standing on windowsills in different parts of the house. I feel that Dick and I have no privacy for our grief.

I am glad to have Ruth with us, though – cheerful and chatty, oblivious of what has happened to her uncle. When Anne arrives at 9.30 and takes over, we discuss the possible arrangements for baby-sitting during the funeral. As always, she offers to help out in any way she can. Once again, I remind myself how lucky we are to have her – as we are also to have Victoria, who shares the nanny role with her.

There are other calls to make. I talk to my mother and tell her the latest plans for the funeral. She has spoken to Mark, who says they will all return from France early; it is the mad August rush back to Paris this weekend, the most dangerous time to drive in France. They are keen for the funeral to be later rather than sooner. I tell her I am driving down to Sussex and will be seeing her that afternoon, and that Colin will be coming to Wiblings to discuss the funeral.

When the phone rings once more it is Mark, telephoning from France. He and his family are staying with friends in the south-west. It is Tommy's birthday. In a typically blunt manner, he asks if John died of natural causes. I am shocked by what I take to be the implications of his question and snap back at him.

'Of course he did!' But I feel rattled, as if Mark knows of my murderous feelings towards John the previous day. Mark says that they will be back in time for a funeral on Wednesday, not before.

I am annoyed by being told when to organise the funeral. 'I don't know yet what day it will be. It may be Tuesday, it may be

Wednesday. We'll just have to see when Colin can get us in,' I say, airily. 'The crematorium is very busy.' Is everyone else going to start telling me whether a day or time is convenient?

After I hang up, Colin calls. Fortunately for Mark, the funeral is to be at 2.30 on Wednesday 31 August at Islington Crematorium in East Finchley.

Adam comes to collect me in Kenny's grey BMW sports car and we drive over to Islington. On the way to the house, he warns me that there may be some discussion about the funeral; Jacques has some ideas about it that may not tally with mine.

When we arrive, Imogen, Jacques and Paul are already there. We make some coffee and go over the events of the previous night; then I talk about the funeral. I explain again that Colin is calling in a favour from someone at the Co-op, and that John will stay in London rather than being taken all the way down to Chichester and back. I give them the name and telephone number of Colin's contact, and say that on Wednesday Colin's hearses will come up to London, pick John up from the Chapel of Rest (I can barely say these words without putting on a silly voice) and take him up to the crematorium where everyone will congregate. There will be no procession; we shall just make our way there by car. I tell them that Dick will put John's chosen music on to a tape to play at the funeral.

As I speak I can see that Jacques is concerned about something. Then it comes out.

'But what about the Mercedes hearse?' He frowns anxiously.

I glance over at Adam, who looks quickly away.

'What Mercedes hearse?' I try to control the bossy big-sister tone creeping into my voice.

'A few weeks ago, John and I walked down Upper Street

and there was a big black Mercedes hearse parked in the road. John said that he wanted that at his funeral. He said he wanted to be sent off in fine style.'

This is tricky. Again I find myself annoyed by John's extravagant ideas. Of course, it would be fine to have a fantasy about such a hearse – and finer still to be able to afford one. But unfortunately, Jacques had taken him at his word.

'I'm not sure, Jacques,' I say gently. 'This is the first time I've heard about the Mercedes hearse. John never mentioned it, even though he asked Dick and me to arrange his funeral. I should think it's very expensive, and I don't know that my mother would be too pleased about paying for it.'

Looking at Jacques' face makes me think that the words are not sinking in. Colin has quoted us a price for the basic modest funeral our family would expect. Since John has no estate, the thousand-odd-pound bill will have to be paid for by my parents, probably my mother, and running up expenses hiring fancy cars is not something Mum would appreciate.

In the awkward silence that follows, I feel that Jacques thinks we are being cheap; we are not giving John the send-off he deserves. I also feel, as before, that Jacques believes there is plenty of money in our family and that we are being stingy.

Now is not the time to be blunt about this. I do not want to hurt Jacques' feelings, or to have a fight.

'It would complicate things using a Mercedes hearse owned by another undertaker,' I point out, 'when all the arrangements have been agreed with Colin. But I could see what he has to say,' I add hurriedly, and telephone Colin straight away.

Luckily Colin is at his office. I explain the situation; I tell him that there is a request for a Mercedes hearse and ask him what he thinks about this. He hesitates before speaking.

'We don't have a Mercedes hearse ourselves,' he says, 'we

have silver Volvos. And to be quite honest, I don't think the extra expense would be worth it.'

He hesitates again, waiting for my response.

'Thank you,' I say. 'That answers my question.'

I put down the phone and repeat what Colin has said. The matter is now sorted out, but it could have been difficult.

Moments later we see a black transit van pull into the road and park a few yards up. Soon the doorbell rings and we all go to answer it. The undertaker on the doorstep looks like a character out of a Dickens novel, with his dark suit and lugubrious face. Another man stands behind him.

The undertaker is clearly confused about who is watching him as he comes in. 'Mrs Dally?'

I step forward and nod. Does this man know in advance what people have died of? Presumably they take precautions against AIDS, or perhaps they take precautions whatever the cause.

'And where is the deceased resting?'

He is talking about John. Suddenly my brother has a new title – the deceased. From the diseased to the deceased, from dead to resting. The euphemisms make my skin crawl.

I climb the stairs ahead of them. Jacques follows behind.

One of the undertakers lifts the sheet. There John lies, grey and naked. 'Would you like us to dress him? Do you have particular clothes you would like him to wear?' Their faces are without expression. I don't know how to talk to them, they give me no clues.

Suddenly I am acutely conscious of John's nakedness and I feel guilty about telling David not to dress him. Do these strange men think that he has been neglected? Do they think we are not treating him with respect?

Jacques goes to the wardrobe. I don't know if he is annoyed or not as he pulls out a pair of dark grey cotton trousers.

'These are his Paul Smith trousers,' he says. 'He was fond of them.' His voice is about to crack as he hands the trousers to the undertaker and then rummages around in the wardrobe a little more before pulling out a rumpled white Gap shirt.

'I expect the trousers are too big now. This shirt needs to be ironed. It won't take long.' He disappears.

I wait on the landing, unable to make small talk with the undertakers. Normally I would quiz them about their trade, but they are doing their job and it would be wrong to ask them to distance themselves. And it would appear unfeeling to step out of my own bereaved role and start asking questions about their work.

The wait seems like an eternity as I stand and watch, aware of the two men standing stiffly by John's bed. From the next room I can hear the swish of the water in the steam iron as Jacques pushes it backwards and forwards over the shirt. The noise is intermingled with the sound of his sniffing as if he is trying to hold back tears.

When he returns, with the shirt reasonably ironed, Jacques goes back to the wardrobe and pulls out a dark suit. 'This is his Armani suit. It's his favourite.' He rushes his words, holding back tears.

The undertakers take the clothes. Jacques and I go downstairs and wait with the others while the men prepare John's rigid body.

Ten minutes later, one of the men comes down. 'The deceased is ready, if anyone would like to pay their respects.'

Imogen has made out the death certificate, which she hands to the undertaker. She has written 'AIDS' as the cause of death.

This is getting increasingly unreal. We all get to our feet and slowly climb upstairs.

The sight is horrible. Against the stark whiteness of the shirt, John's skin looks grey. He seems to be shrinking by the minute – swamped by the expensive designer suit which only a year ago he filled with his strapping, fit body. I can look for only a moment before I turn away.

We return to the sitting room, red-eyed and sniffly. The joking has stopped; this is suddenly serious as we sit and wait.

Five minutes later, the undertakers come down, carrying John in a black body bag on a stretcher. I always associate body bags with young men killed in battle. We shall see him no more. The final never-again.

They carry him out of the house and down the steps. As Imogen shuts the door, we all let out a wail of grief and hug each other.

The house immediately seems empty. With John gone, we no longer have a reason to be there. Besides, there are things to do and we go our various ways. Imogen and Paul must go to work. Adam and I must register the death. I'm not sure if Jacques is going to work or not.

Adam and I drive down to the register office in Clerkenwell. We are mainly silent, but we do laugh ruefully about the Mercedes hearse. Typical of John, we agree. On the way, Adam picks up John's will from the solicitor.

The Registrar, a big man in his late fifties, has a gentle manner as he takes down the details of John's life. The death of my young brother is registered in my name and I sign the documents for posterity. The details of John's death are now public.

Adam drives me back to Kentish Town. I have an urgent need to be at home with Dick and Ruth. I miss Rebecca and Alice, too, and would love to have them with me. At the same time, I am glad that I do not have to handle their grief as well as my own. Dick and I decide that we shall tell them when they return from America, after the funeral.

After lunch, I drive down to Wiblings with Ruth. At teatime, Colin comes over to discuss the final details for the funeral. My mother greets him; she remembers him when he was at the Midhurst Grammar School with my uncle Edwin, though she last saw him at Simon's funeral five years ago. Colin is a quiet and gentle man with a sympathetic and organised manner. What a strange view of the world undertakers must have. They see us all at our most vulnerable.

The next day, Saturday, Adam drives down from London. The subject of death notices comes up. Unlike Simon, John will have no obituaries, but we shall put notices in the *Guardian* and the *Independent*. We discuss the wording with our mother. They can cost several hundred pounds, these notices, so we want to be succinct.

Dick, Adam and I talked about this the day before. We are convinced that we should state that John died from AIDS. Being gay himself, Adam feels particularly strongly about this, and I want to show that we as a family are not ashamed.

When we discuss this with Mum, she is not so certain. 'One doesn't usually put the cause of death,' she says. 'And AIDS is not the actual cause anyway.'

'Well, Imogen put AIDS as the cause on the death certificate,' I reply, 'and notices often do say that someone died of cancer or a heart attack. It saves people having to ring up to ask what has happened.'

Is my mother embarrassed about the fact that John has died of AIDS? Perhaps she does not want the world to know that he was homosexual. It is unusual for her to care what other people think of her; she is normally so bold and outspoken. I think she is just so devastated that she cannot judge what is the right thing to do. It may simply be the difference in attitude between one generation and another.

Adam is getting agitated and upset. I can see the tension in his neck muscles and know he is reaching the end of his tether. Apart from his own feelings as a gay man, perhaps he thinks our mother's hesitation reflects a difficulty she has with his homosexuality anyway. Who knows?

Whatever the case, he loses his temper but clearly does not know what to do. He gets up, slams the door and drives back to London.

As I watch him go, I feel mournful and left behind. I want to join him but cannot abandon my mother at this point. I resign myself to the idea of a grim weekend of dead silence – the silence of the survivors.

The weather doesn't help the mood; the air is damp and muggy. On Sunday morning I take Oma and Ruth up the Downs at Bignor and, as always, imagine the Roman army marching along Stane Street. Oma is very lame but determined to walk as far as she can. She manages about five hundred yards on her two walking sticks before having to return to the car. When she gets in, she sits panting breathlessly. The wind whips around my head as I stand beside her. We talk about the view, how we can see the curve of East Head in the distance and the sea beyond. We do not talk about John very much. She has seen two grandsons die and she still has two years of life ahead of her. I think she is bewildered by it all, but then so am I.

My grandmother will not be coming to the funeral. She is too old, and the cremation in North London is too far away. My Aunt Barbara will stay with her in Sussex on the day.

Back home in London on Monday, I feel energy surging through my veins. I clear out my old office room at home and start to paint the walls pistachio green – Rebecca's choice for what will be her new bedroom. I listen to the radio and paint for hours, concentrating on the task before me. I want to get it all finished before she returns from America; a welcome-home surprise, to balance the other news.

I feel strange – disassociated but also all-powerful, restless, omnipotent. 'It's the manic defence,' says my mother when I tell her that evening.

I look it up. According to Charles Rycroft in *A Critical Dictionary of Psychoanalysis*, the manic defence is a 'form of defensive behaviour exhibited by persons who defend someone against feelings of anxiety, guilt and depression . . .' Too right, I think.

When Simon died, I took one day off and then worked flat-out for ten days to meet the deadline for a special books supplement I was editing for the magazine. It never occurred to me to take off any more time. I would not have wanted to, I would not have known what to do with my thoughts. It seemed essential at the time, as now, to have practical projects to concentrate on, to keep one's thoughts away from reality.

I cannot stay too far away, though. On Monday Jacques rings me in a panic, sounding very upset. 'John's missing,' he says. 'I rang the number you gave me at the Co-op because I wanted to arrange flowers to go on top of the coffin. They said they know nothing about him.'

I feel accused of neglect. My brother has disappeared and I know nothing about it. I am too tired to react. I tell Jacques I'll get back to him, then I call Colin and leave a message on his machine. Although it is a bank holiday and the office is closed, I know that he will be looking in from time to time to pick up any messages. Sure enough, Colin returns my call within the hour.

Within ten minutes he has sorted out the confusion. John is indeed still there in the Chapel of Rest; but because he is not a Co-op 'client', his name is not on their computer. I ring Jacques and assure him that John is there, that he can go and put flowers on the coffin if he wants. I realise that I have not thought about any details such as flowers, and I have not budgeted for them either. Then Jacques asks about decorating the crematorium for John's service.

'We only have forty minutes, Jacques,' I say. 'In and out. I don't think there will be time for anything like that.'

Dick and I discuss the funeral, how it should be organised, what should be read. We ask Adam if he would like to say or read something. He declines, as does Jacques. I am glad (but not surprised) that Imogen wants to give a little talk.

The next day, Tuesday, I drive to Ikea and buy bookcases which I spend the rest of the day putting together by myself. I also go to the local flooring shop and buy vinyl for the laundry-room floor. Thanks to the manic defence, I manage to do more in two days than I would normally accomplish in a month. Rebecca's bedroom is nearly finished and I have moved into my new study, where I sit at my desk and admire my summer garden through the window. It's so perfect and quiet, I can hardly bear to look for long.

I feel as if I am drifting through this interim between the death and the final goodbye. I felt it when Simon died, too – and that was for a longer period because his suicide automatically meant an inquest had to be held before his body was released for burial. It is a period of unbearable limbo, and deadly boring because you cannot settle, cannot concentrate, cannot laugh. All the humour has seeped out of us. For the time being, there is nothing left.

Imogen comes to supper and shows us the draft for her talk

at the funeral. It includes touching anecdotes of her schooldays with John at St Christopher's. Again I feel sad that she never became my sister-in-law. We talk more about the details of the service and the order of the music and readings. I am to read some lines from Walt Whitman's *Leaves of Grass*; Dick has chosen a poem, *The End*, by the American Mark Strand, and some Housman.

At night I lie on the sitting-room floor and play the music John has chosen for his funeral. The Cat Stevens song reminds me of a period of angst in my own past, when I listened to it after I had split up with a boyfriend at Oxford. I play it over and over again, loudly, listening to its unsophisticated message like an introverted teenager. I can tell that this drives Dick mad (he doesn't like Cat Stevens), but he is too kind to complain. I feel out of control, but in an odd way the music seems to gather me in and hold me. Five years ago, when Simon died, I lay on my back on the floor of the sitting room and cried my heart out to the sound of John Lennon's 'Imagine'. It's becoming a habit.

Chapter Thirteen

The Funeral

I wake early to find myself worrying about what I am going to wear to my brother's funeral. Outside, the air is muggy and damp. Typically, I cannot find any garment that is both suitable and comfortable. I am ashamed to find myself caring: there is so much to do and I am stymied by trivial sartorial decisions. It is absurd, I know, but I do not want to be sweaty and red-faced as I stand up and recite from Walt Whitman. I am beginning to wish that I had not agreed to recite anything. I don't even know if I understand these lines well enough to read them properly.

In the end I wear a safe black linen jacket, white blouse and short black and white check skirt. All the black seems funereal, which is not what I am intending, but there it is. At work most people wear black; the majority of my clothes are black. Fashion lends a hand to funeral-goers.

The moment Anne arrives, I leave Ruth with her and go to Woolworth's. There I buy fifty paper plates, plastic cups and napkins. I have no idea how many to cater for. You don't ask people to RSVP to a funeral, so you can only guess how many will turn up. Since the wake is not in our house, I have to be as efficient as possible and plan accordingly. I want as little effort for me, and as little inconvenience to Jacques, as possible. We have already agreed to pay Anne and Victoria to set out the food while we are all at the funeral and then to clear up afterwards, as well as care for whichever children need looking after.

The manager serves me. He is a keen young man who looks as though he is on a training scheme, on his way towards a career in Woolworth's, and he is enjoying a stint in the Kentish Town branch to familiarise himself with the day-to-day customers. Bursting with energy and cheerfulness, as his fingers tap out the prices on the till he is almost whistling.

'Having a party, are we?' he asks.

A young man at the beginning of his career. He is younger than John, but his life flashes before me – a middle manager, promotion to senior levels. Wife, children, mortgage, house in the suburbs, golf. He will live to old age, unlike my brother.

I smile at him and answer, 'No, a funeral.'

It is mean of me. The smile freezes on this nice young man's face and he quickly stuffs my purchases into a plastic bag. There is no more banter, no more exchanges between us. I have killed all that good humour and spoiled his day.

Next stop is Sainsbury in Camden. I take the car down the road and rush round the store like the winner of a competition given five minutes to grab as much as possible. Fifty sandwiches with different fillings, bottles of mineral water, orange juice for the children. It's not going to be a fancy spread, but I have no time to think of extra frills. I just want to make sure there will be a reasonable amount for people to eat and drink; it is difficult enough organising all this in someone else's house from a distance. I load up the car and drive the whole lot over to Canonbury where I stuff as much as possible into the fridge.

Concentrating on these practical matters, I keep my feelings under control. I have now practised reading the Walt Whitman lines several times. Until I have read them at the funeral, however, I cannot relax. Dick has worked out the order of the music and readings. The timing is tight; we only have forty minutes.

After lunch, Dick and I drive Ruth and Anne over to the house, where they will stay during the funeral. Ruth is too young to understand what is happening and I see no point in her coming. If she were older, I would want her with us.

Anne will also be looking after Jane's three-year-old son Matthew during the funeral. Jane has just arrived from France and joins us in the car, driving up through North London to the St Pancras and Islington Cemetery in East Finchley. We hardly talk.

The cemetery is a vast area, nearly two hundred acres of rampant undergrowth, stretches of cut grass and mature trees. Narrow, winding roads pass Victorian tombs and gravestones. Within the grounds there is an Anglican chapel and a Roman Catholic chapel, as well as the crematorium which was built much later in the 1930s. There is something wild and wonderful about this surprising place, surrounded as it is by busy highways and suburban terraces. It has a dreamy, gentle atmosphere which has probably been there since it was first established over a hundred years ago.

As we pull up, we can see the silver Volvo hearse by the door. I wonder briefly if Jacques is still cross about the Mercedes. The coffin lies in the back. As I imagine John's body lying inside that box, my throat seizes up. Quickly, I rummage in my bag to check for the umpteenth time that I have the tape of John's music.

Dick and I check out the sound system, which is a tape recorder situated in an anteroom. After a few panicky minutes, we work out which level to put the music on to and, more or less, how to fade it in and out.

We have very little time to do anything now. People are arriving. My uncle Edwin and his wife, Anne; my cousins. Many faces I don't recognise, friends of John – young men, some looking well, some looking ill. All looking sad. Friends of my parents appear, including Tilly Edelman who had a special relationship with John as a little boy. My mother used to play tennis with Tilly and her husband Maurice, an MP, years ago. When Winston Churchill died in 1965, Maurice took my mother and me to see him lying in state. I was eleven, and I can remember Maurice taking my arm in a gentlemanly manner, making me feel for the first time that I was a young woman rather than a girl. Although Maurice died a long time ago, Tilly remains a warm, engaging woman who can talk to anyone of any age. She is old, but she has managed to come to John's funeral.

It is nearly 3.30. The coffin has been carried in and placed on the platform in front of the seats. It is covered with a magnificent display of white flowers – organised by Jacques with blooms from Azagury Fleurs, the flower business John and Adam set up in the good old days, before everything started to go wrong.

I sit in the front row next to Jacques. There are Imogen and Paul, Robbie and David. The room is filling up. I see Adam and Kenny, who is trying not to be recognised in dark glasses, a hat and a dreary grey raincoat. (He told Dick, who complimented him on his sunglasses, that they were 'celebrity shades'.)

Mark and Clare arrive with their three children. I see Debbie Postgate, and other friends, and one of the nurses from the palliative care team appears at the back. It is touching to see her and I wonder was John special to her? Or does she go to the funerals of all her charges?

Dick puts on the first piece of music chosen by John, the Gypsy Kings. By the time it has finished, the crematorium is packed. The doors are closed, there are people standing squashed in at the back. John had a lot of friends. There is a hush in the room, and everyone seems tearful.

The poems are read: Housman, Mark Strand and Walt Whitman. I read my lines fluently, but I wobble a bit with the intonation. As I say the last words, my control goes and I scuttle back to my seat as the emotion bubbles up. Next comes the Cat Stevens song about parental neglect. It is crass, but it is John's choice. I reflect that it must have been hard being the third boy and the fifth child in a family of six.

I glance at my parents on the other side of the aisle. My mother, Philip and Peter are all sitting together. Anne Norwich, ever tactful, has seated herself a few places away. They all stare ahead, looking stunned. Are they listening to the words? It seems unlikely, given how much they disliked all our pop music when we were teenagers. Who knows what they are thinking?

I am thinking how awful it must be for them to be burying another child, but at least there are a lot of us. One advantage of coming from a big family is that there are plenty of others left when someone dies, I suppose.

Dick asks us to stand to sing 'Jerusalem'. He tells everyone that John suggested this as it was the only hymn he knew. People chuckle gently. We stand and our sad and wistful singing is nearly drowned out by the powerful notes of the organ.

Now it is Imogen's turn. She gives a warm and engaging

talk about her friendship with John and what it was like for her to be with him both as a friend and as his doctor. She has known him since they were fourteen. Her speech is loving and funny and it makes people smile to hear descriptions of John as he truly was, and the pranks he got up to at school. It also makes us cry. She describes John's early entrepreneurial talents. 'At school he would serve breakfast in bed for a small fee!'

People laugh softly. I know that the eggs and bacon in these breakfasts had been collected from the doorsteps of the good people of Letchworth in the early morning – but Imogen, the head girl, never knew that. It is a funny secret.

Imogen talks about how John retained his humour and interest in sex right to the end, and she describes a moment last week when she was having to sort out his bedding and Jacques offered to help: 'John smiled and said, "Oh, Jacques, you just want to have a fiddle."'

Our time is nearly over. Imogen sits down and I put on John's final choice – the Mozart 'Jesu Domine'. As this music soars around the room the blue curtains slowly come together, hiding the flower-decked coffin behind them.

We, the audience, sit there listening to the painfully exquisite music until it is over. Then there is silence apart from the sound of quiet sobbing. Jacques and I hug each other.

Dick stands up and thanks everybody for coming. As people start to leave, my mother asks him to invite everyone back to the house in Canonbury.

We exit from the grey building to a grey sky outside. Straggly groups of people look at the wreaths and bunches of flowers laid out on the ground for John. Others stand around looking awkward. What do you say after a funeral for a young person?

Another group of mourners are arriving for the next funeral. We have had our slot and now it is someone else's turn. I am reminded of Simon's funeral at the Chichester crematorium five years ago. That was a busy place, and they were shunting one family in through one door as they ushered another family out through another. When we arrived, I saw a familiar face among the mourners exiting from the earlier service – Bianca, an old friend of my mother, had got there early and mistakenly walked into someone else's funeral. By the time she realised that she was mourning a stranger, it was too late to leave; she then had to come round to the entrance again and sit through Simon's funeral.

Kenny says goodbye. He will not be coming to the house but we have invited him to supper on Friday. Otherwise, most people are coming back. We drive back down the Archway Road and on to Canonbury. The weather is foul – cold and drizzly.

Back at Alwyne Road, Victoria is there and has arranged all the food and drink ready for the guests. Matthew and Ruth have been playing well together; they run around, looking for the startled cat. Tsar, wisely, has disappeared. The house fills up with people. Suddenly everyone is ravenous. The sandwiches rapidly disappear and the drink goes down fast. Paul and Dick go out to buy another case of wine. When they return, I know it is time to leave. The energy has drained from my body; the manic defence has gone, leaving me feeling weak and depressed.

My parents are leaving too, as are the older guests and relatives. It is time for just John's friends to be together in his house.

My mother wants Adam, Dick and me to meet later for supper at Mark and Clare's house in Hampstead, where Jane and Matthew are staying the night. She wants her surviving children gathered together. Adam declines, but I reluctantly agree to go. I would prefer to stay at home with Dick, but I can see it means so much to her that we agree.

The evening is strained. Philip and Dick drive to the Thai restaurant in Kentish Town to get a take-away, but the service is slow and they have to wait for an hour. At the house we sit waiting for them to return. Apart from the children, no one speaks. We adults sit in the sitting room. After a funeral there is so little to say. I long to be released to climb into bed and escape from the day.

Things are made even worse by the fact that Mark is not feeling well and has taken to his bed. Clare is worried, and with reason. His old leg injury from the motorcycle accident over a decade ago has left him with chronic osteomyelitis, infection of the bone and bone marrow in his leg, which flares up now and then. On the day of his younger brother's funeral it has erupted again. The following day he is in the orthopaedic ward at the Royal Free Hospital on an intravenous drip while my mother spends the next few days believing that she may lose another son. If this were a novel, it would be implausible and absurd.

Finally Dick and Philip return with the food, which we eat quickly so that we can leave. We say goodbye to Jane, who is returning to France with Matthew the next day, and drive home to fall, exhausted, into bed. It has been a draining day; I feel as if I have been sapped of all energy.

The following day, too, Rebecca and Alice return from New York. Dick goes to the airport to collect them. On the tube coming back into London, they ask, 'How's John?' When Dick tells them that their uncle has died, they cry and get angry. They wanted to come to the funeral, they say. They miss John, they loved John.

When they arrive home and I try to comfort them, I do not
know if we were right to postpone telling them until now. I can
justify it in some ways, but there are arguments on both sides.
I am aware that the strongest reason for me is purely selfish; it
is easier to deal with my own grief without having to deal with
theirs as well. Now that the funeral is over, I can give my children attention. At my most cynical, I think that they are most
upset about having missed a family occasion.

The next day I do not telephone anyone in the family. After
the intensity of the past few weeks, I need to withdraw and
enjoy time with Rebecca, Alice and Ruth. No one calls me, so
I am probably not alone in feeling that way. The family has
been smashed apart again. It will be some time before it can be
reconstructed in any form.

Chapter Fourteen

September

On Thursday, Adam collects John's ashes from the crematorium and arranges to drive down to Sussex with Kenny the following day. Before he died, John asked Adam to scatter his ashes in one of the fields there.

I was surprised and touched to hear this. It seems that John had a feeling that he wanted to come home and be with his family and with his dead brother Simon, whose ashes are also there along with our grandfather's.

I sensed a note of anxiety in Adam's voice when he first told me this, and immediately after the funeral it does seem prudent to get the ashes before Jacques does. Apparently Jacques has said he wants to keep them himself. We chuckle at the idea of my brother's soft white ashes and bits of bone sitting on a mantelpiece in a North London flat or wherever Jacques will move to when the bank has repossessed the house. I used to think it was only a joke that people kept the ashes of their loved ones at home, but now I know it's true. And who am I to laugh? I still have my section of Simon's skull tucked away among my shirts and jumpers.

It is odd that John, who left no messages and made no bequests to anyone, should make this request. It may have been for sentimental reasons but it could also be that, right to the end, he was still playing Adam and Jacques off against the other. He promised Jacques money but not his body. The significance is lost on Jacques, who says that he wants to be present when the ashes are scattered.

That Friday evening, when Adam comes to supper with Kenny and Kenny's boyfriend, a handsome dark young Italian called Freddie, we hear about the day's events.

Adam and Kenny drove down to Wiblings in one car, Jacques and David in another, arriving in time for lunch with Philip, my stepfather. I sense that Adam was annoyed about this. I think he wanted to be by himself when he finally said goodbye to John's body. They had a remarkable brotherly relationship, inseparable for over thirty years – a relationship which in all the drama of the past few months has never been properly acknowledged. Adam never says it either, but I know that on a day-to-day level he will miss John far more and for longer than anyone else.

My mother was in London, so Philip was alone at Wiblings when the four men arrived. The food was on the table, Philip opened a bottle of wine and they sat down for a pleasant meal, warding off any attempts to be maudlin. Kenny set the scene, telling joke after joke until they were all nearly sick with laughter.

After lunch the party set off for the field next to the house. Adam carried the heavy plastic urn in his arms. Kenny's manic joke-cracking at lunch was now under control as he allowed himself to reflect for a few moments.

Philip has planted many new trees on the Wiblings land, especially after the 1987 storm. Several of these have been planted in honour of one grandchild or another. In the second Wiblings field, there is a young oak tree surrounded by strong wooden bars to fend off the bark-stripping deer. This is Alice's tree; she was born exactly a month after the 'Great Storm', and on the day of the King's Cross fire.

Jacques had the idea that they should walk all the way around the two-acre field, dropping a handful of ashes every now and then as they went. Philip, who had already measured the field, gently suggested that they would run out of ashes before walking even half-way round. Far better, he suggested, to put them all at the foot of Alice's tree. That way they are together and they will, over time, be washed down to the roots and provide vital nutrients to help it grow and thrive.

Jacques fortunately saw the sense in this – or, at least, did not argue.

The ritual over, they then drove back to London, John's remains left in Sussex around the trunk of the young tree that will see us all out.

At Falkland Road, the evening is relaxed as our conversation moves away from John and Jacques and the funeral. Kenny is manic but highly intelligent and wildly amusing. He regales us with stories about his Catholic upbringing in Liverpool.

'I hope I don't beg for the priest on my death-bed,' he says.

We eat outside in the garden, but as the temperature drops we move inside for coffee in the sitting room. Kenny looks at our floor-to-ceiling bookshelves and becomes serious, almost morose. He says that the sight of all these books makes him feel intellectually inferior. 'I never read books,' he says, 'but I want to. Tell me what I should read.'

We talk about short stories and tell him that he would probably enjoy the works of William Trevor. I have recently finished reading the whole collection of his stories in a hardback edition. I cannot imagine that any sensitive person would fail to respond to them, even if he 'isn't a reader'. I write my name in the book and hand it to him.

John's ashes lie in the field, and the eight-month drama is coming to an end. Now we have to get back to normal. After living on tenterhooks for so long, ordinary life will seem dull.

Adam goes back to New York; I return to work, relieved that Linda is back in charge. With the uncertainty of each day gone, I can get on with work on the magazine in a mindless sort of way. Fired once again with the manic defence, I go to book parties after work – one for Erica Jong, another for Julie Myerson, a big one for Ruth Rendell. I feel like a robot at these events. Sometimes I mention John, sometimes I don't. One day, the numbness will lift.

Outside work, I use every spare moment to finish my book, this novel that I have written while John was dying. In some ways I think it was what kept me going through it all – the commitment to meet a deadline, and the ability to create a world over which I had full control. I think I am pleased with it, but every other day I panic about whether it is good enough.

Since John's death, I have been concerned about Jacques' welfare and ring him periodically to see how he is. I often speak to David, who tells me that Jacques is bearing up. But now – the moment we've been dreading – there is trouble over John's will.

First Jacques complains to me that Adam has not shown anyone the will and that he does not trust him. I have not seen

John's will either, but I do believe Adam when he tells me that everything was left to him. Their business affairs were complicated and they had always ensured that if anything happened to one of them, the other would take over everything. I have no reason to believe that John has left Jacques anything in his will, which was written some years ago.

One evening Jacques telephones me at home. Sounding upset and angry, he suggests that Adam is robbing him of whatever he is owed. I feel sad for him; he evidently cannot believe that John has not remembered him. Since I have not seen the document, I cannot confirm that Adam is right; but I try to assure Jacques that if indeed John has left him anything,. Adam would not be allowed to take it. That would be illegal and not easy to do, since the other executor to the will is a lawyer.

A few days later, I hear rumours from other members of the family that Adam is not being straight about John's will. I suspect Jacques has been telephoning them, too, in an attempt to enlist their support. I feel that I've been shoved in the middle of this squabble, and it annoys me. When I telephone Adam, he agrees to fax copies of the will to us – but he is damned if he will send one to Jacques. He says that Jacques has refused to give him any of John's personal belongings – not even a favourite jacket – to remember him by. It has reached a childish level. I think of my father's elephants and the headless Egyptian cat, knowing we shall never see them, either. The only things I have of John's are the CDs he chose for us to play at his funeral. I have to concentrate on what matters, and make myself not care. It's only now, years later, that I realise how sad and angry I am about this.

The faxed will arrives and it is very simple: everything is left to Adam. I pass that information on to Jacques next time I call. I am still trying to be kind to him and support him, but I sense a petulance in his voice as if he thinks I'm not doing enough, that I'm not on his side. And of course, if he wants to draw up a line between himself and Adam, I shall not be on his side.

Early October sees a climax at work. On Monday, 1 October, the managing director Terry Mansfield takes me out to lunch at his club. I have had a few run-ins with Terry in the past and am anxious about spending an hour and a half with him. However, in spite of his tough business reputation, he is renowned for his extraordinary kindness when people have personal problems.

Terry is in kind mode. As we are driven in his Mercedes to Berkeley Square, he tells me that he has been thinking about my family tragedy. He sounds genuine and I am touched. Later at lunch he tells me a private story of his own about a death in his family, which brings me close to tears. I am amazed that he can be so open, but I also feel that I am not yet strong enough to take in such a sad story.

Then Terry switches the conversation, and the true reason for our lunch quickly becomes apparent. He asks me if I would be interested in becoming the book publisher for the company, to develop books for the magazines. He tells me that I know more about books than anyone else in the firm, and he thinks I would be suitable for what he needs.

I am interested. I have often thought that I know how the company should go about publishing books. But at the moment I am aware that I have no energy inside me. I am not in a fit state to take on a new and responsible job.

'It wouldn't happen straight away,' he says. 'It would be some time next year.'

Next year? Well, I will have recovered my strength by then, I think, and my enthusiasm for work. But I am cautious. They might not give me the job anyway.

'Well, if you advertised such a job,' I say, 'I would apply.'

My conversation with Terry perks me up. Suddenly I see a future for myself within the company. I outgrew *Cosmo* and moved on to *She*. Now I am aware of coming to the end of my time at *She*; five years is long enough on any one magazine. I know I don't want to be a magazine editor, so my prospects as a journalist are not likely to fit with my own ambitions and my need to have a stimulating and challenging job. Now there is something interesting facing me in the future.

That evening, I come home feeling quite buoyant. But my mood is to change when I find a letter from a debt-collecting agency for Marks & Spencer awaiting me.

Since I was the one who registered John's death, my name is on the records. The letter expresses condolences for my sad loss and then demands the £5,000 which John had borrowed from them and failed to repay. When the bank refused to continue lending to him, he evidently borrowed from every other possible source. M. & S. launched their financial services at around that time, and John was in there obtaining as much credit as possible.

My rage frightens me. Not only am I angry with John for being so greedy and irresponsible; I wonder how many more of these letters I shall receive. I am also livid at the insensitivity of Marks & Spencer.

As I am re-reading the demand, Jacques telephones and says that he has just received the same letter. He tells me they both borrowed money from Marks & Spencer; it was John's idea, apparently.

'But you signed,' I say harshly. The two of them were just hopeless. Jacques would do anything John asked him to do, and John took advantage of that fact.

But Jacques' call is also about something else. He is ringing to tell me that his house has been broken into and that his Filofax with all his contacts has been stolen.

'What's that got to do with me?' I ask.

He proceeds to allege that Adam must have organised the break-in.

I am astounded. Is Jacques going insane? 'But Adam's in New York,' I say, 'and anyway, why would he want your Filofax?'

'I know he's behind it,' Jacques insists. 'He knows how to organise such things. I spoke to your mother about it; I told her, too.'

Now I lose my temper.

'Jacques, don't you realise that we have all lost John, we are all bereaved? It's not only you. My mother has lost two sons and you are accusing another one of organising a break-in from New York. Just think of others for a change, will you? I appreciate you have financial problems but you must take some responsibility for that, you know. You and John were both signatories on the mortgage; you both defaulted on the payments years ago, and that's why you're losing the house. You lived a good life on lots of money and it caught up with you. John borrowed from everyone and his debts have to be paid off. I'm afraid my mother's house is more important to me than your welfare, Jacques. You are a grown man.'

Everything I have held back over the months comes out and I can almost feel my rage flowing down the telephone line. Jacques can feel it; he slams down the phone and that is the last time we speak.

John's ashes lie in the Sussex field and we are still affected by the fall-out from his life.

A few weeks later, Jacques writes to Anne Norwich to complain about my mother's and my shameful behaviour towards him. But Anne writes a sweet note in return, saying simply that she understands that he is upset in his grief. She sends me a copy of this letter to Jacques. We have closed ranks.

With the letter, Anne encloses prints of the photographs she took of John earlier in the year. They are haunting portraits of a thin young man who stares sadly into the camera. Anne is a graphic artist and she has also drawn several portraits of John – early in the year, then later when he was in bed in the summer. She has given them to me, and these are the closest I have to the photographs I wish I had taken at the time.

When Simon died, obituaries in the *Guardian* and the *Independent* placed my eldest brother's achievements in the public domain. There is no such public memory of John, but the rest of us who saw him grow up constantly remember him. He remains alive in conversations with my parents and siblings, and with his friends – both as the tall, charming man with his naïve but original outlook on life and as the passive creature wasting away in bed. John never raged against the dying of the light, which made it easier for the rest of us in the end. But when I am alone and I remember his miserable last days, his tears of fear, the wretchedness of his condition, I feel an intensely painful sadness at his loss, as though some crucial component of my family's history has been ripped out and thrown away.

When this happens, it is easier to recall the other memories of John – as the big grinning baby on my six-year-old hip, or the skinny little boy in his grey school shorts. There is also John as a teenager, John the prankster and John as a generous young adult when he was successful – and richer than anyone else in the family. It was then that he was sure of himself for the first time in his life. He was happy with his sexuality and happily accepted for it. He had succeeded in spite of his dyslexia, and he had reason to be proud of that after having spent so many years of his life feeling a failure.

All his life John was irresponsible and reckless, and he left a mess behind him when he died. But I believe the mess he created was prompted more by a natural impulse to please others than by malice. He was simply incapable of recognising that it is not always possible to make everyone love you, and that his efforts to do so caused irrevocable damage to several relationships.

When Simon died it felt as though the family had been smashed apart, flung to different corners of our worlds to pick ourselves up and recover as much as anyone can after the shock of a suicide. There is a photograph that Dick took of me and the girls, moments before we walked into Wiblings to find Simon lying dead on the grass. That image marks the end of my old world.

Over the months, some of us slowly came back together but the family was changed for ever. However, happy events followed. Ruth was born, as were my nephews and nieces. We all entered a new phase of life.

John's death shattered us all again but it was different. This time we knew it was coming and we had time to brace ourselves. But it came fast on the heels of Simon's death, and no babies have been born into the family since. Perhaps this makes it seem sadder.

No family deserves the loss of any young member, let alone two. Perhaps people who lose their sons in wartime feel the same sense of injustice. There was, however, in the months running up to John's death, a sense of togetherness. In their own way people chipped in to show John support, visiting him and taking part in his death, as they had taken part in his life. So in spite of the unfairness of another death, once we had re-established the patterns of our daily lives, I think the family was closer. In some ghastly way, the tragedy had strengthened old ties and created new links between the survivors.

Five years on, I feel not only a closer link with my own family but also a special bond with others who have lost a loved one in tragic circumstances. Just as having your first baby brings you into the hitherto unknown world of parenthood, so losing a child, partner, sibling or young parent opens the gates to the sorrowful world of the bereaved. This is a place you can never leave.